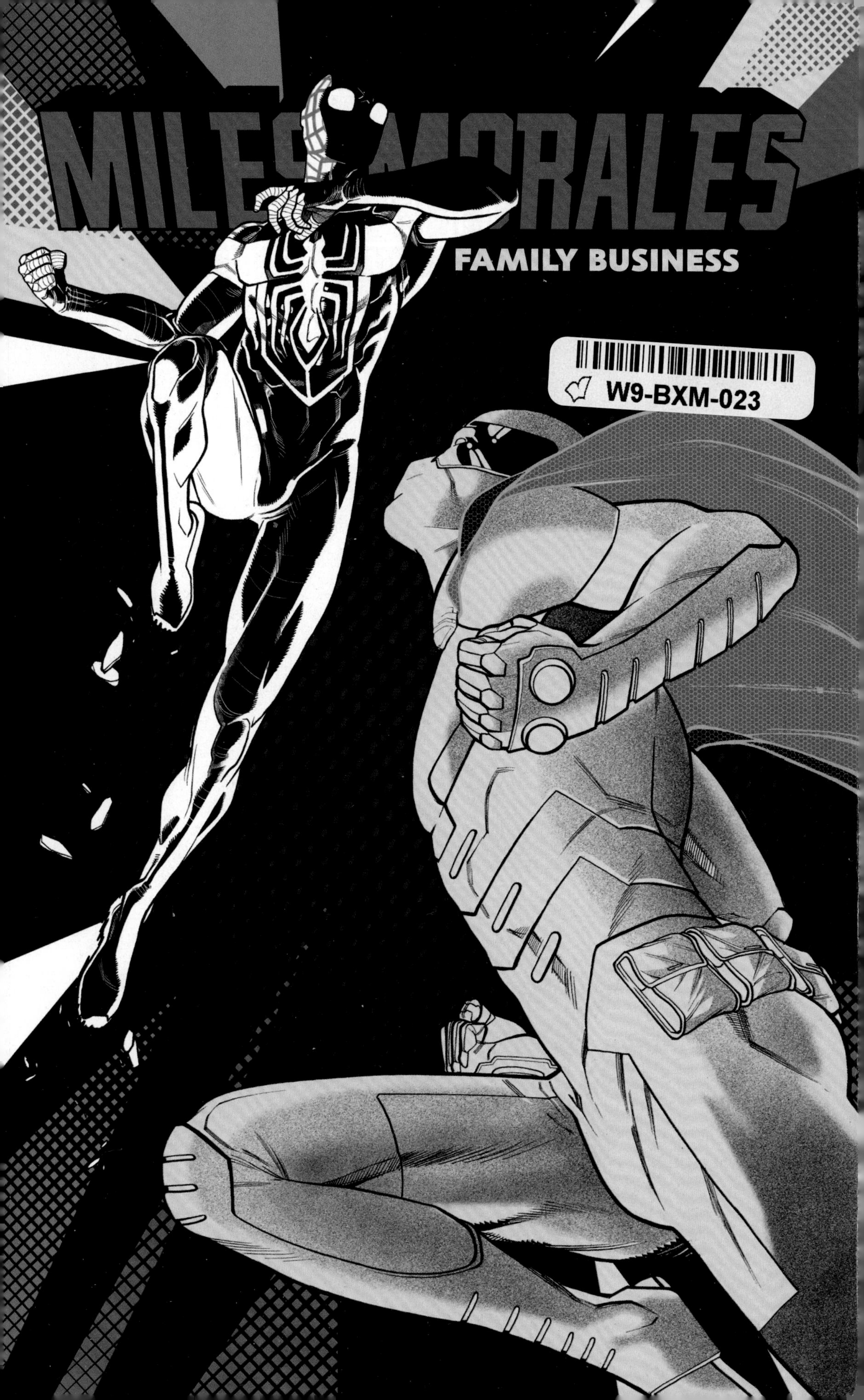
MILES MORALES
FAMILY BUSINESS

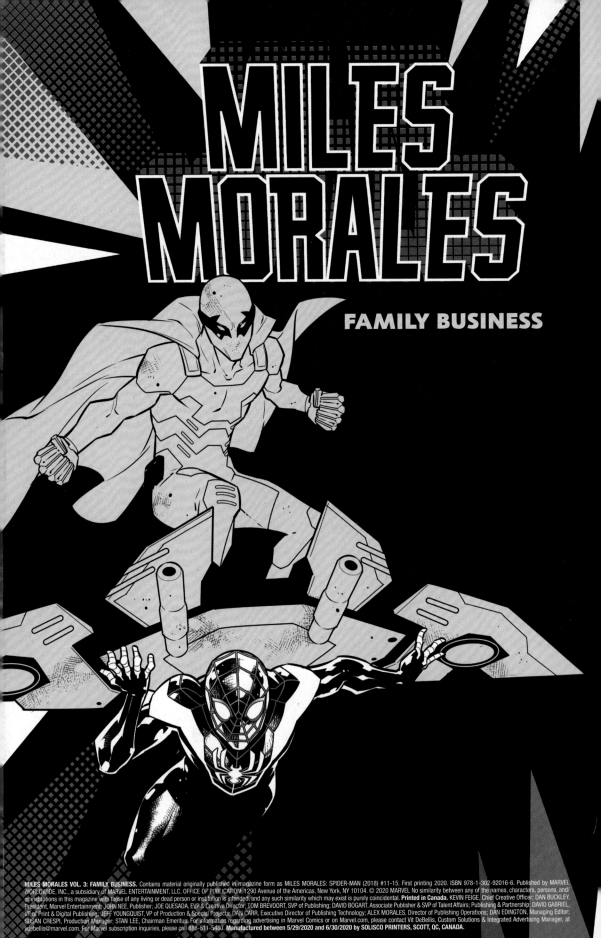

MILES MORALES

FAMILY BUSINESS

MILES MORALES VOL. 3: FAMILY BUSINESS. Contains material originally published in magazine form as MILES MORALES: SPIDER-MAN (2018) #11-15. First printing 2020. ISBN 978-1-302-92016-6. Published by MARVEL WORLDWIDE, INC., a subsidiary of MARVEL ENTERTAINMENT, LLC. OFFICE OF PUBLICATION: 1290 Avenue of the Americas, New York, NY 10104. © 2020 MARVEL No similarity between any of the names, characters, persons, and/ or institutions in this magazine with those of any living or dead person or institution is intended, and any such similarity which may exist is purely coincidental. **Printed in Canada.** KEVIN FEIGE, Chief Creative Officer; DAN BUCKLEY, President, Marvel Entertainment; JOHN NEE, Publisher; JOE QUESADA, EVP & Creative Director; TOM BREVOORT, SVP of Publishing; DAVID BOGART, Associate Publisher & SVP of Talent Affairs; Publishing & Partnership; DAVID GABRIEL, VP of Print & Digital Publishing; JEFF YOUNGQUIST, VP of Production & Special Projects; DAN CARR, Executive Director of Publishing Technology; ALEX MORALES, Director of Publishing Operations; DAN EDINGTON, Managing Editor; SUSAN CRESPI, Production Manager; STAN LEE, Chairman Emeritus. For information regarding advertising in Marvel Comics or on Marvel.com, please contact Vit DeBellis, Custom Solutions & Integrated Advertising Manager, at vdebellis@marvel.com. For Marvel subscription inquiries, please call 888-511-5480. **Manufactured between 5/29/2020 and 6/30/2020 by SOLISCO PRINTERS, SCOTT, QC, CANADA.**

10 9 8 7 6 5 4 3 2 1

Saladin Ahmed
WRITER

Zé Carlos (#11, #14), Ig Guara (#11),
Javier Garrón (#12-13, #15),
Kevin Libranda (#13),
Alitha E. Martinez (#13),
Ray-Anthony Height (#14) &
Belén Ortega (#14)
ARTISTS

Dono Sánchez-Almara (#11),
Protobunker (#11, #13) &
David Curiel (#12-15)
COLOR ARTISTS

VC's Cory Petit
LETTERER

Mike Hawthorne & David Curiel (#11);
Ken Lashley & David Curiel (#12);
AND Javier Garrón & David Curiel (#13-15)
COVER ART

Lindsey Cohick	Kathleen Wisneski	Nick Lowe
ASSISTANT EDITOR	EDITOR	EXECUTIVE EDITOR

SPIDER-MAN CREATED BY Stan Lee & Steve Ditko

COLLECTION EDITOR **JENNIFER GRÜNWALD**
ASSISTANT MANAGING EDITOR **MAIA LOY**
ASSISTANT MANAGING EDITOR **LISA MONTALBANO**
EDITOR, SPECIAL PROJECTS **MARK D. BEAZLEY**
VP PRODUCTION & SPECIAL PROJECTS **JEFF YOUNGQUIST**
BOOK DESIGNERS **SALENA MAHINA**
WITH **JAY BOWEN** AND **MANNY MEDEROS**
SVP PRINT, SALES & MARKETING **DAVID GABRIEL**
EDITOR IN CHIEF **C.B. CEBULSKI**

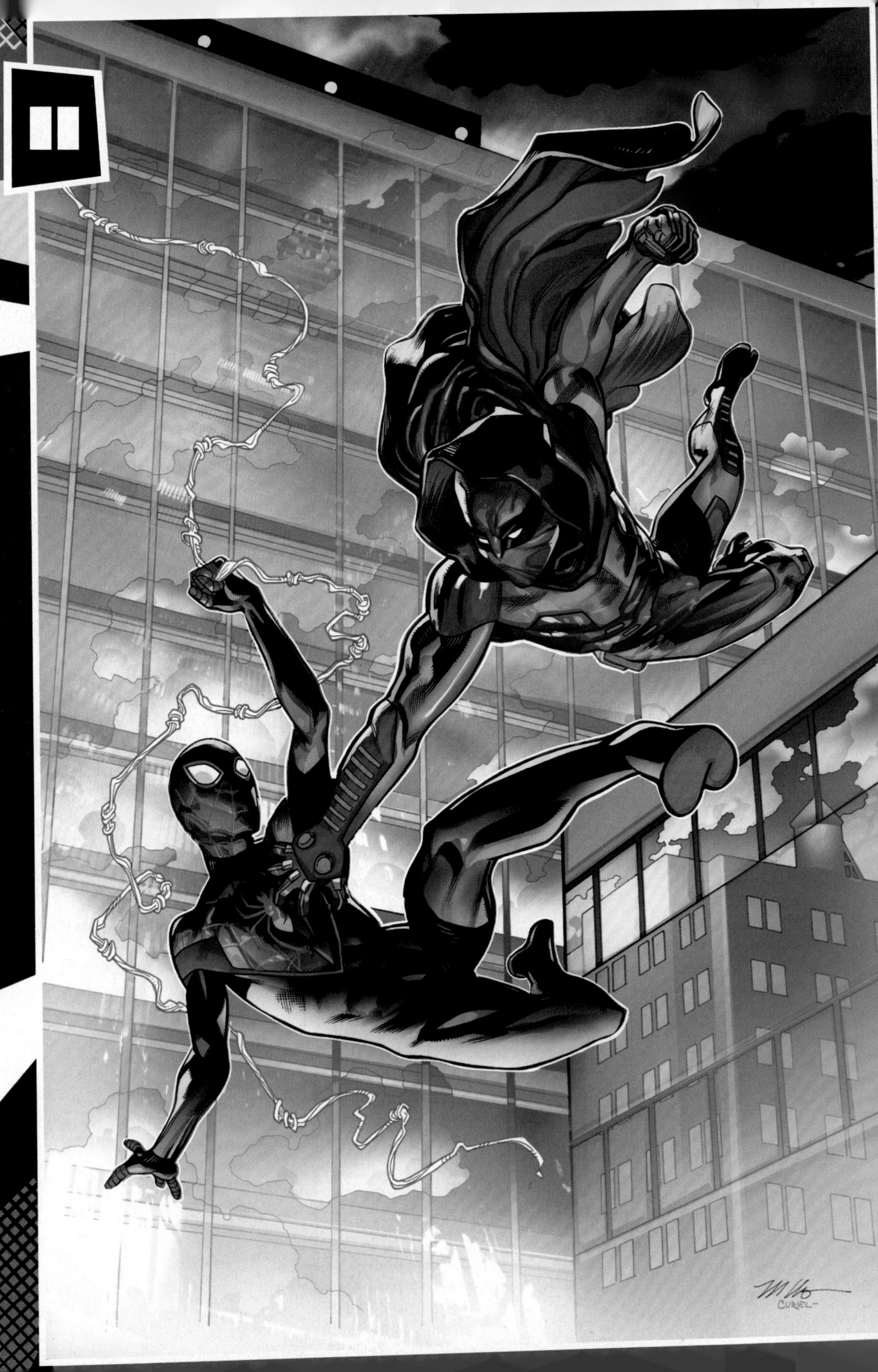

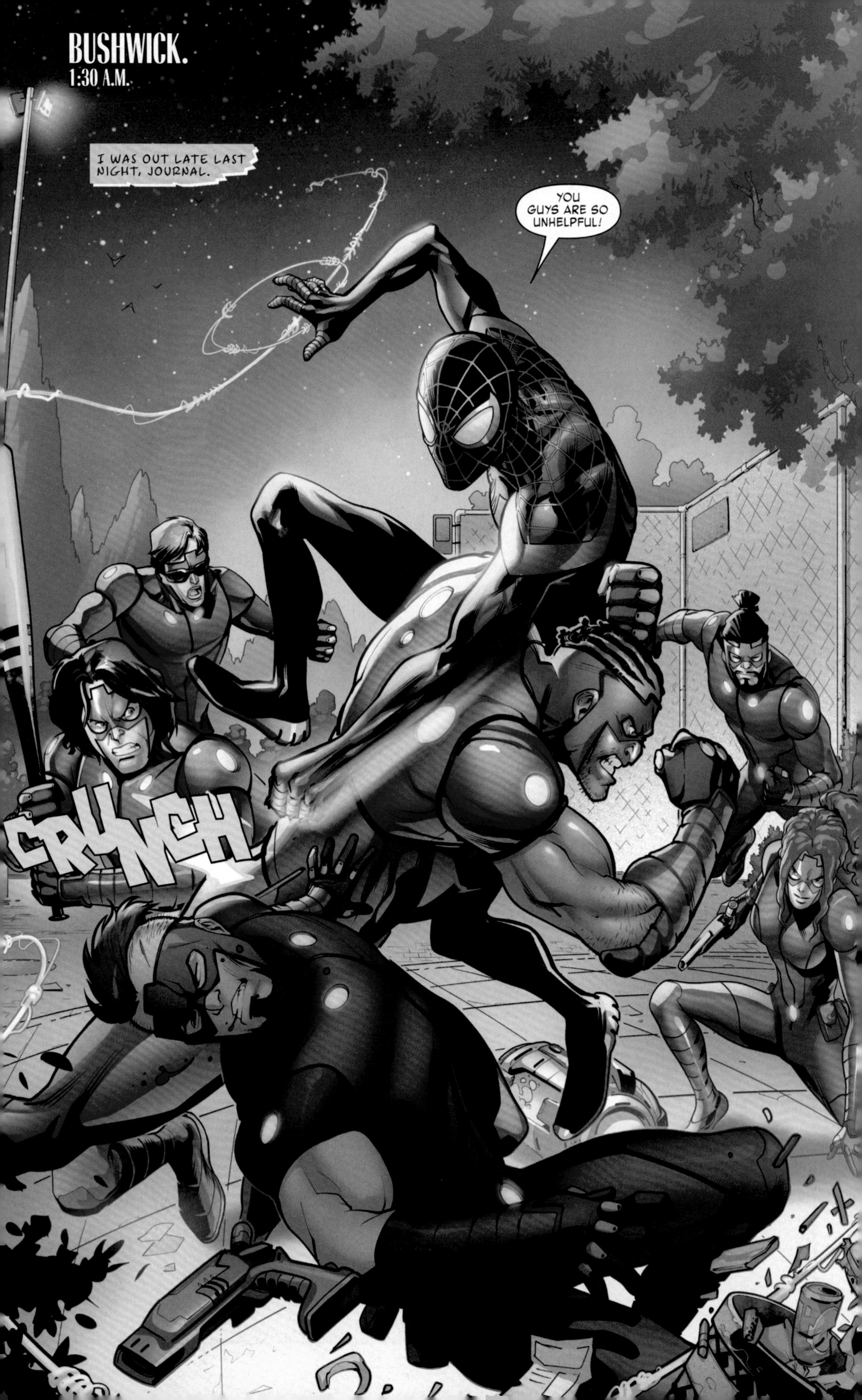
BUSHWICK.
1:30 A.M.
I WAS OUT LATE LAST NIGHT, JOURNAL.
YOU GUYS ARE SO UNHELPFUL!
CRUNCH

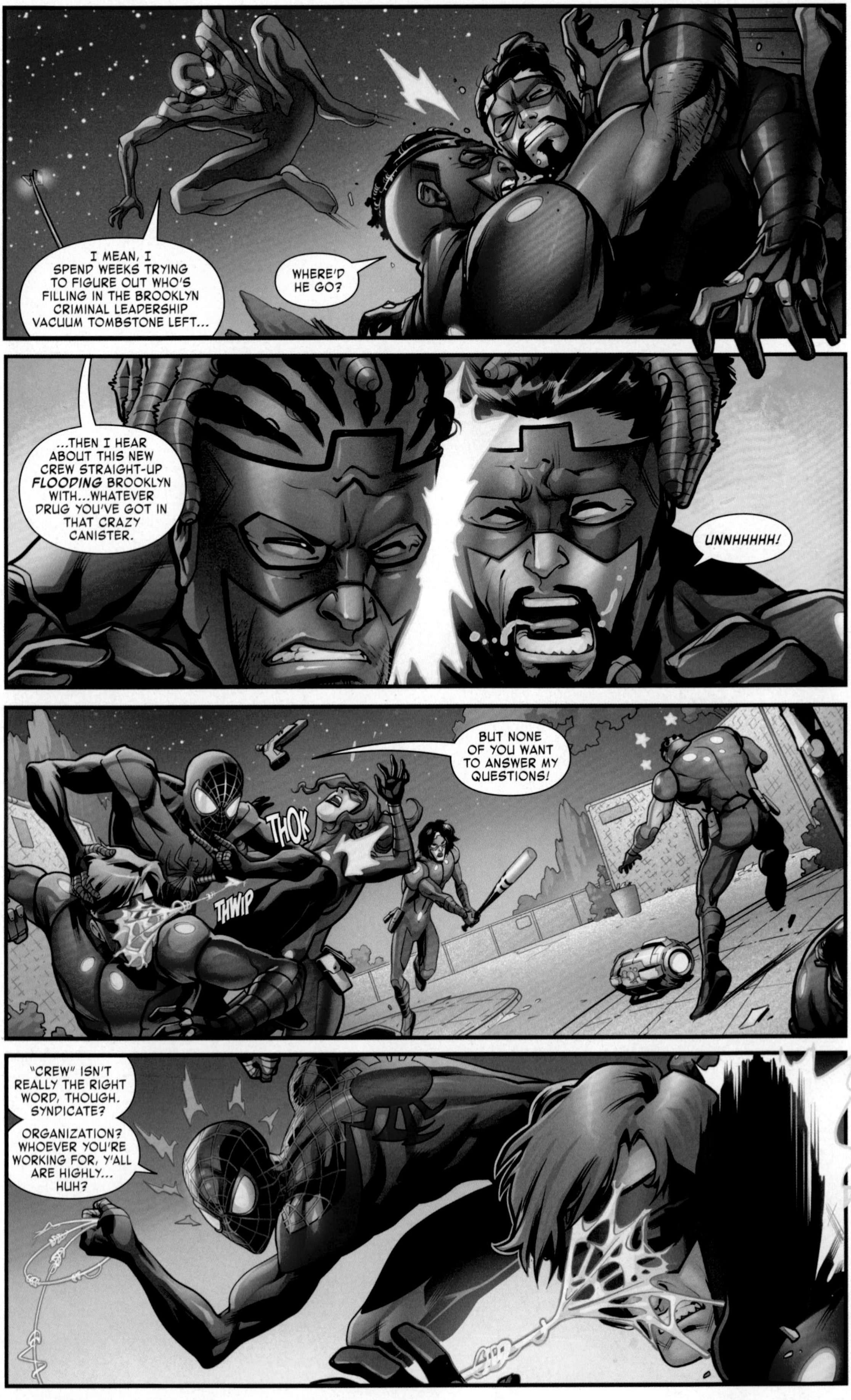
I MEAN, I SPEND WEEKS TRYING TO FIGURE OUT WHO'S FILLING IN THE BROOKLYN CRIMINAL LEADERSHIP VACUUM TOMBSTONE LEFT...
WHERE'D HE GO?
...THEN I HEAR ABOUT THIS NEW CREW STRAIGHT-UP *FLOODING* BROOKLYN WITH...WHATEVER DRUG YOU'VE GOT IN THAT CRAZY CANISTER.
UNNHHHHH!
BUT NONE OF YOU WANT TO ANSWER MY QUESTIONS!
THOK
THWIP
"CREW" ISN'T REALLY THE RIGHT WORD, THOUGH. SYNDICATE?
ORGANIZATION? WHOEVER YOU'RE WORKING FOR, Y'ALL ARE HIGHLY... HUH?

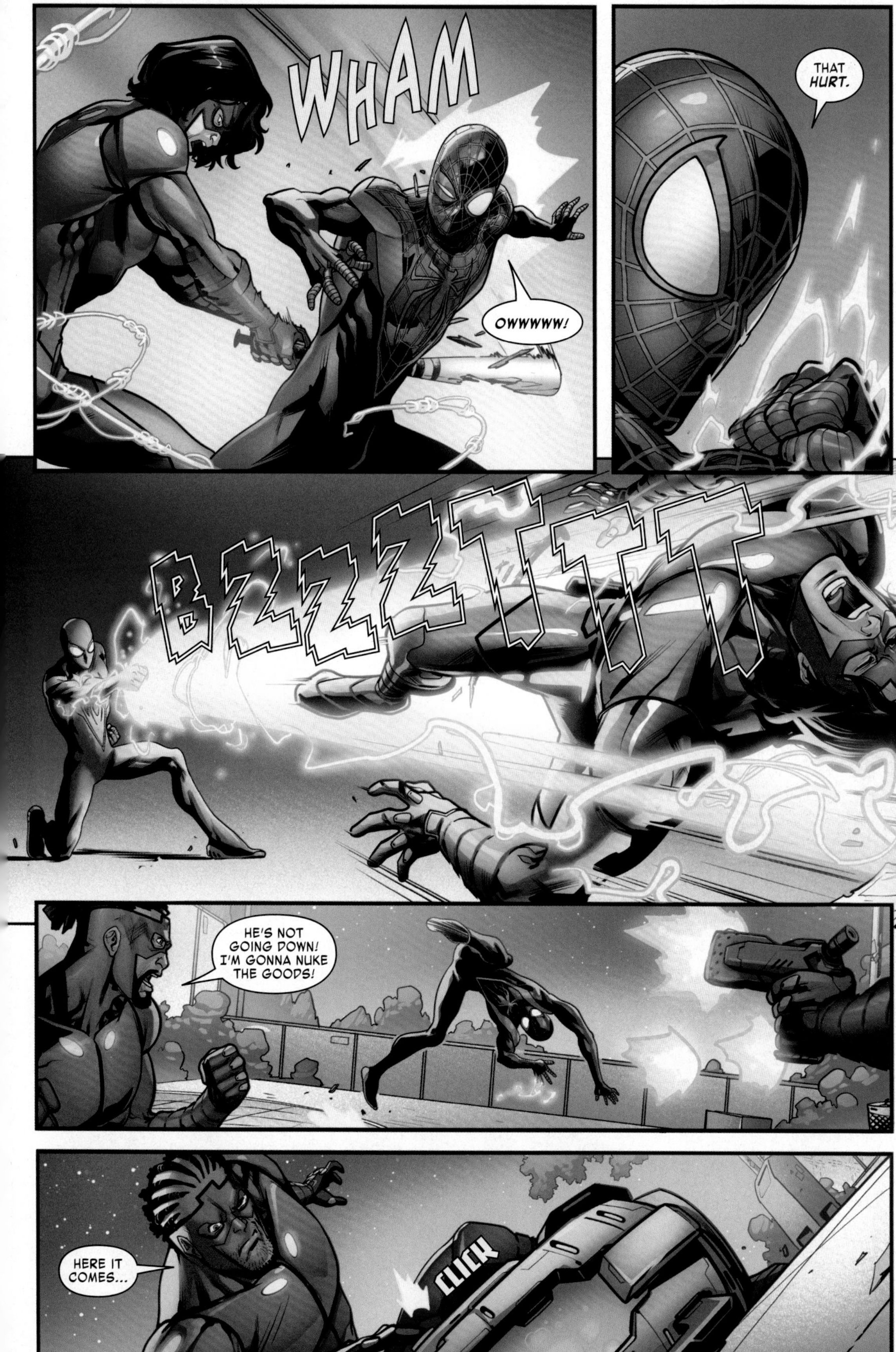
WHAM
OWWWWW!
THAT HURT.
BZZZTTT
HE'S NOT GOING DOWN! I'M GONNA NUKE THE GOODS!
HERE IT COMES...
CLICK

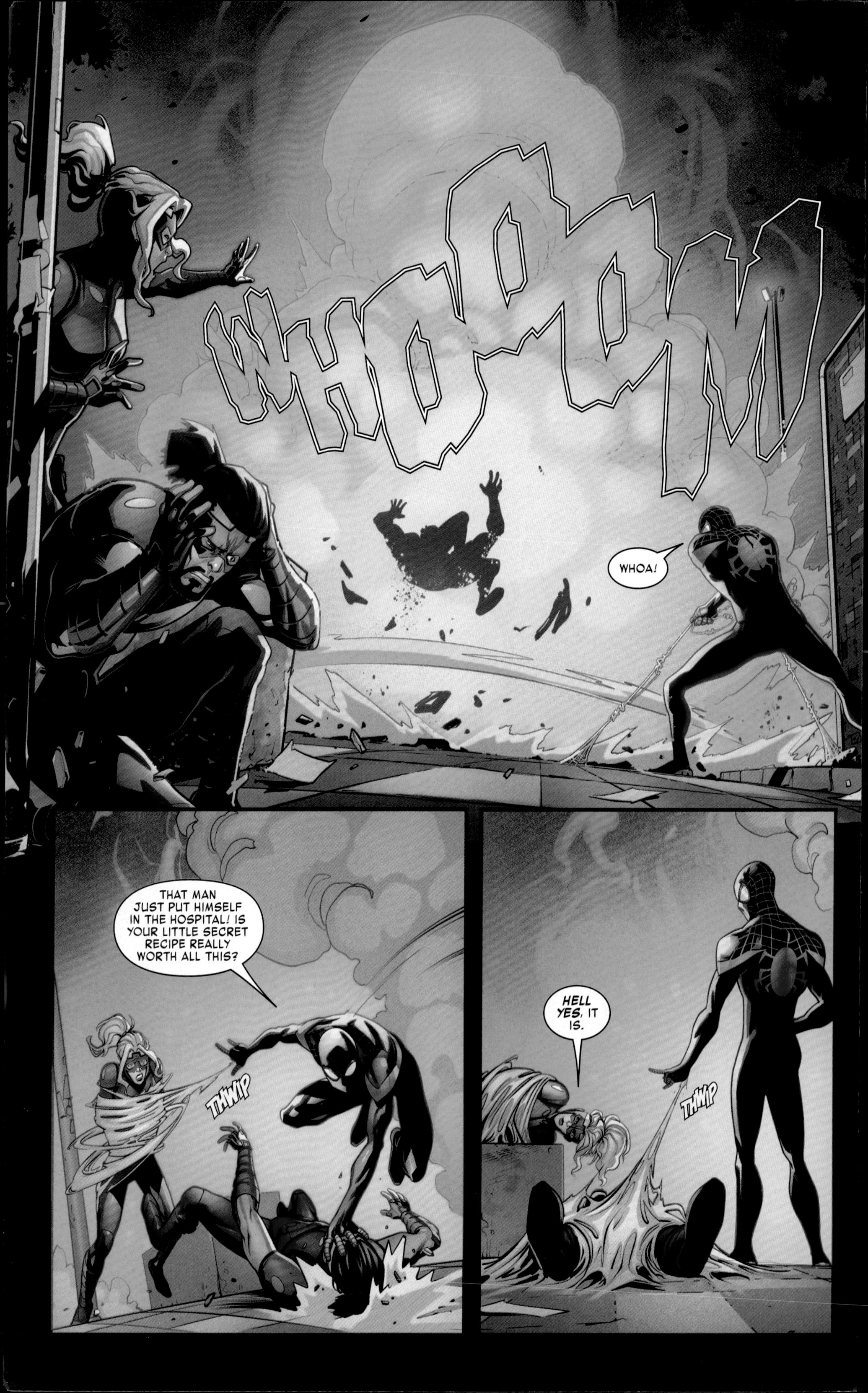
WHOOOM
WHOA!
THAT MAN JUST PUT HIMSELF IN THE HOSPITAL! IS YOUR LITTLE SECRET RECIPE REALLY WORTH ALL THIS?
THWIP
HELL YES, IT IS.
THWIP

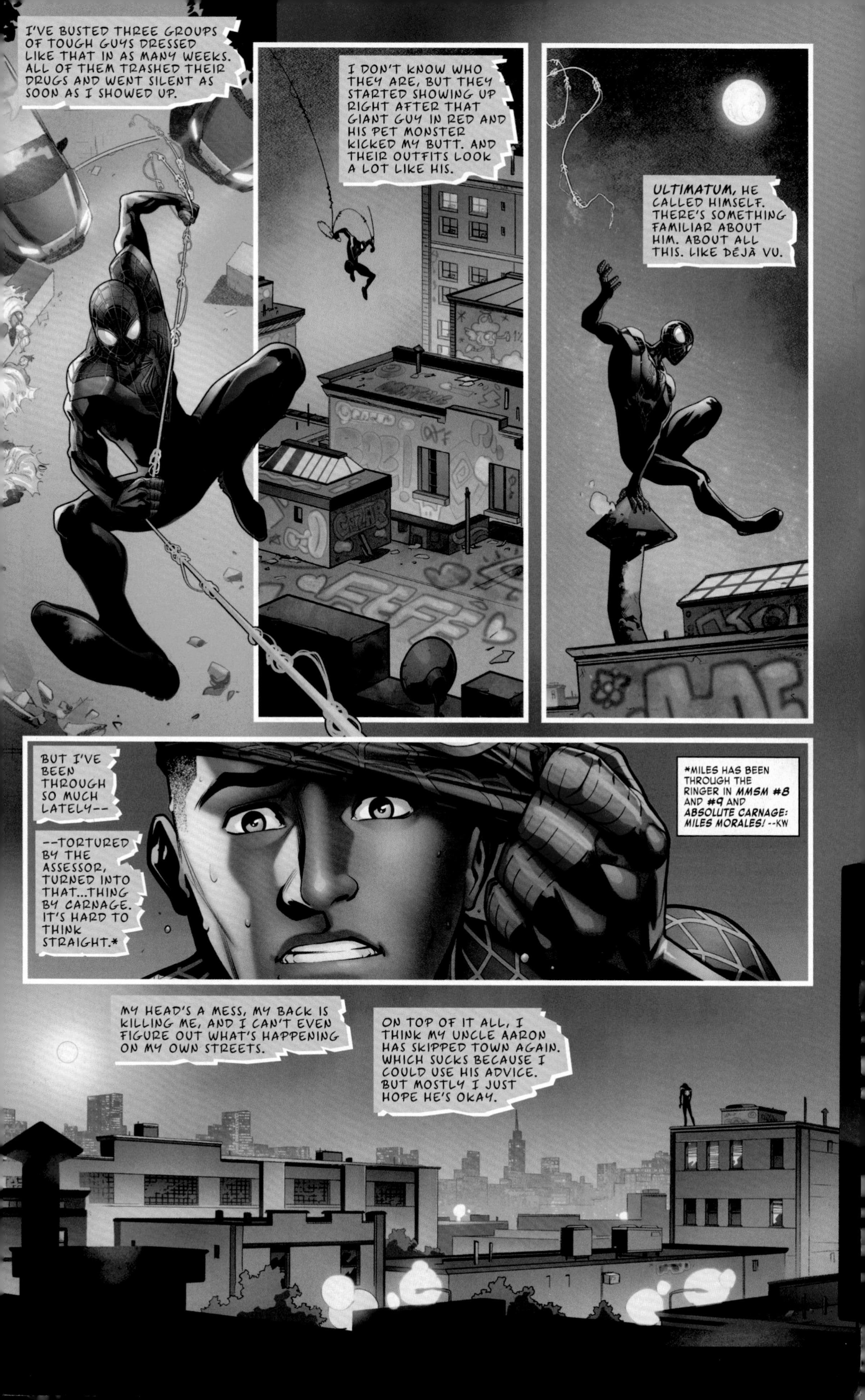
I'VE BUSTED THREE GROUPS OF TOUGH GUYS DRESSED LIKE THAT IN AS MANY WEEKS. ALL OF THEM TRASHED THEIR DRUGS AND WENT SILENT AS SOON AS I SHOWED UP.
I DON'T KNOW WHO THEY ARE, BUT THEY STARTED SHOWING UP RIGHT AFTER THAT GIANT GUY IN RED AND HIS PET MONSTER KICKED MY BUTT. AND THEIR OUTFITS LOOK A LOT LIKE HIS.
ULTIMATUM, HE CALLED HIMSELF. THERE'S SOMETHING FAMILIAR ABOUT HIM. ABOUT ALL THIS. LIKE DÉJÀ VU.
BUT I'VE BEEN THROUGH SO MUCH LATELY--
--TORTURED BY THE ASSESSOR, TURNED INTO THAT...THING BY CARNAGE. IT'S HARD TO THINK STRAIGHT.*
*MILES HAS BEEN THROUGH THE RINGER IN MMSM #8 AND #9 AND ABSOLUTE CARNAGE: MILES MORALES! --KW
MY HEAD'S A MESS, MY BACK IS KILLING ME, AND I CAN'T EVEN FIGURE OUT WHAT'S HAPPENING ON MY OWN STREETS.
ON TOP OF IT ALL, I THINK MY UNCLE AARON HAS SKIPPED TOWN AGAIN. WHICH SUCKS BECAUSE I COULD USE HIS ADVICE. BUT MOSTLY I JUST HOPE HE'S OKAY.

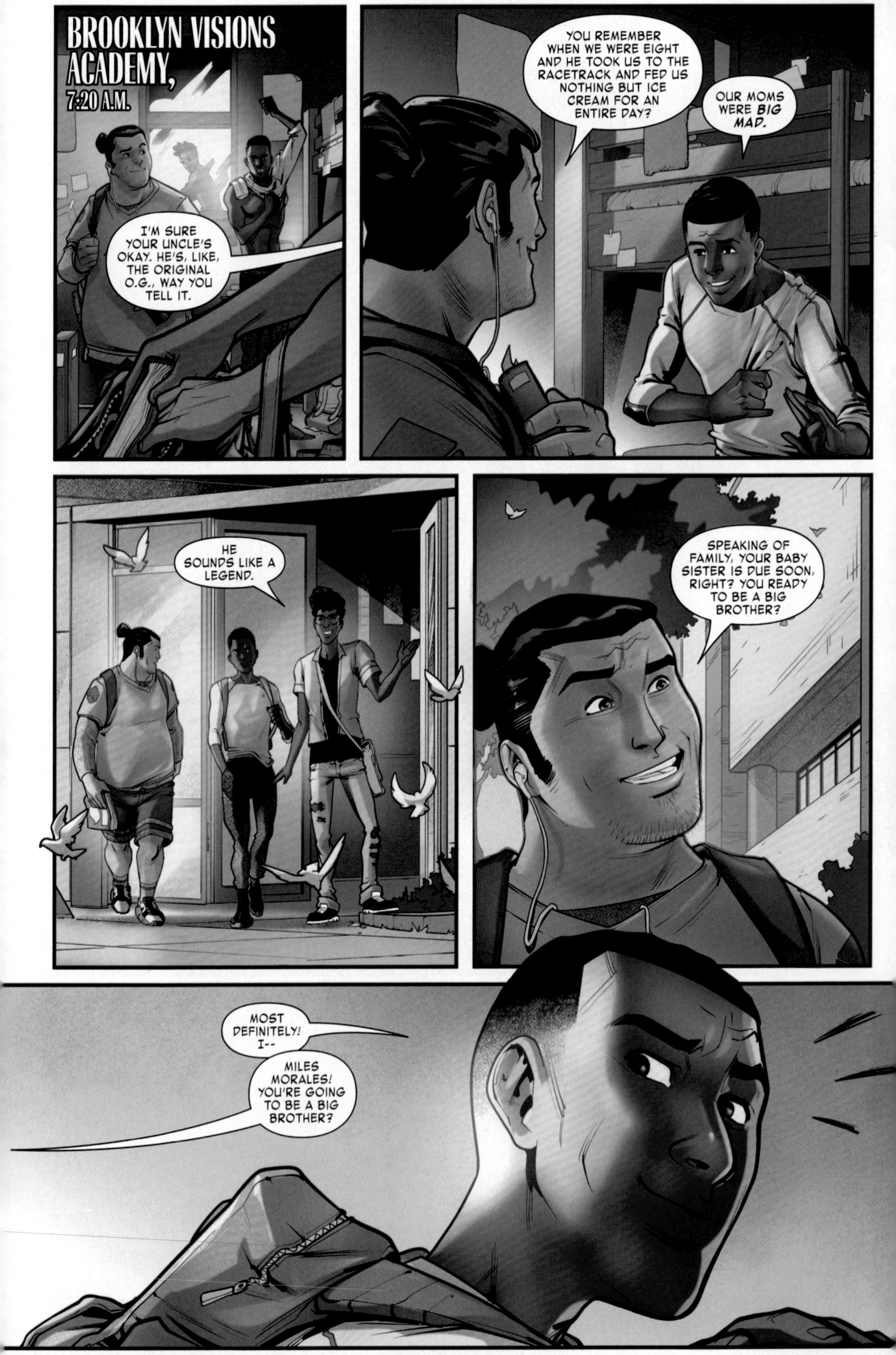
BROOKLYN VISIONS ACADEMY, 7:20 A.M.
I'M SURE YOUR UNCLE'S OKAY. HE'S, LIKE, THE ORIGINAL O.G., WAY YOU TELL IT.
YOU REMEMBER WHEN WE WERE EIGHT AND HE TOOK US TO THE RACETRACK AND FED US NOTHING BUT ICE CREAM FOR AN ENTIRE DAY?
OUR MOMS WERE BIG MAD.
HE SOUNDS LIKE A LEGEND.
SPEAKING OF FAMILY, YOUR BABY SISTER IS DUE SOON, RIGHT? YOU READY TO BE A BIG BROTHER?
MOST DEFINITELY! I--
MILES MORALES! YOU'RE GOING TO BE A BIG BROTHER?

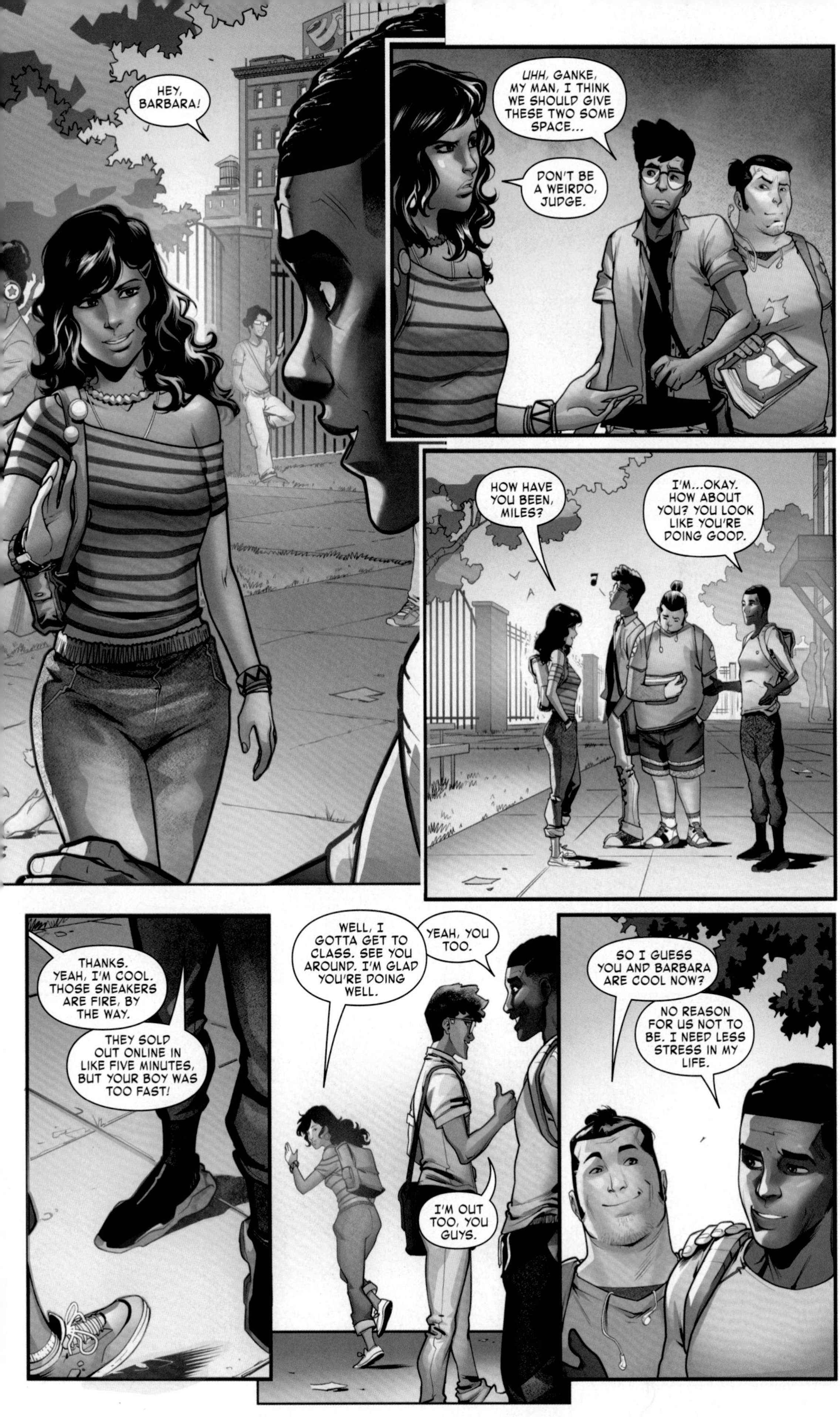
HEY, BARBARA!
UHH, GANKE, MY MAN, I THINK WE SHOULD GIVE THESE TWO SOME SPACE...
DON'T BE A WEIRDO, JUDGE.
HOW HAVE YOU BEEN, MILES?
I'M...OKAY. HOW ABOUT YOU? YOU LOOK LIKE YOU'RE DOING GOOD.
THANKS. YEAH, I'M COOL. THOSE SNEAKERS ARE FIRE, BY THE WAY.
THEY SOLD OUT ONLINE IN LIKE FIVE MINUTES, BUT YOUR BOY WAS TOO FAST!
WELL, I GOTTA GET TO CLASS. SEE YOU AROUND. I'M GLAD YOU'RE DOING WELL.
YEAH, YOU TOO.
I'M OUT TOO, YOU GUYS.
SO I GUESS YOU AND BARBARA ARE COOL NOW?
NO REASON FOR US NOT TO BE. I NEED LESS STRESS IN MY LIFE.

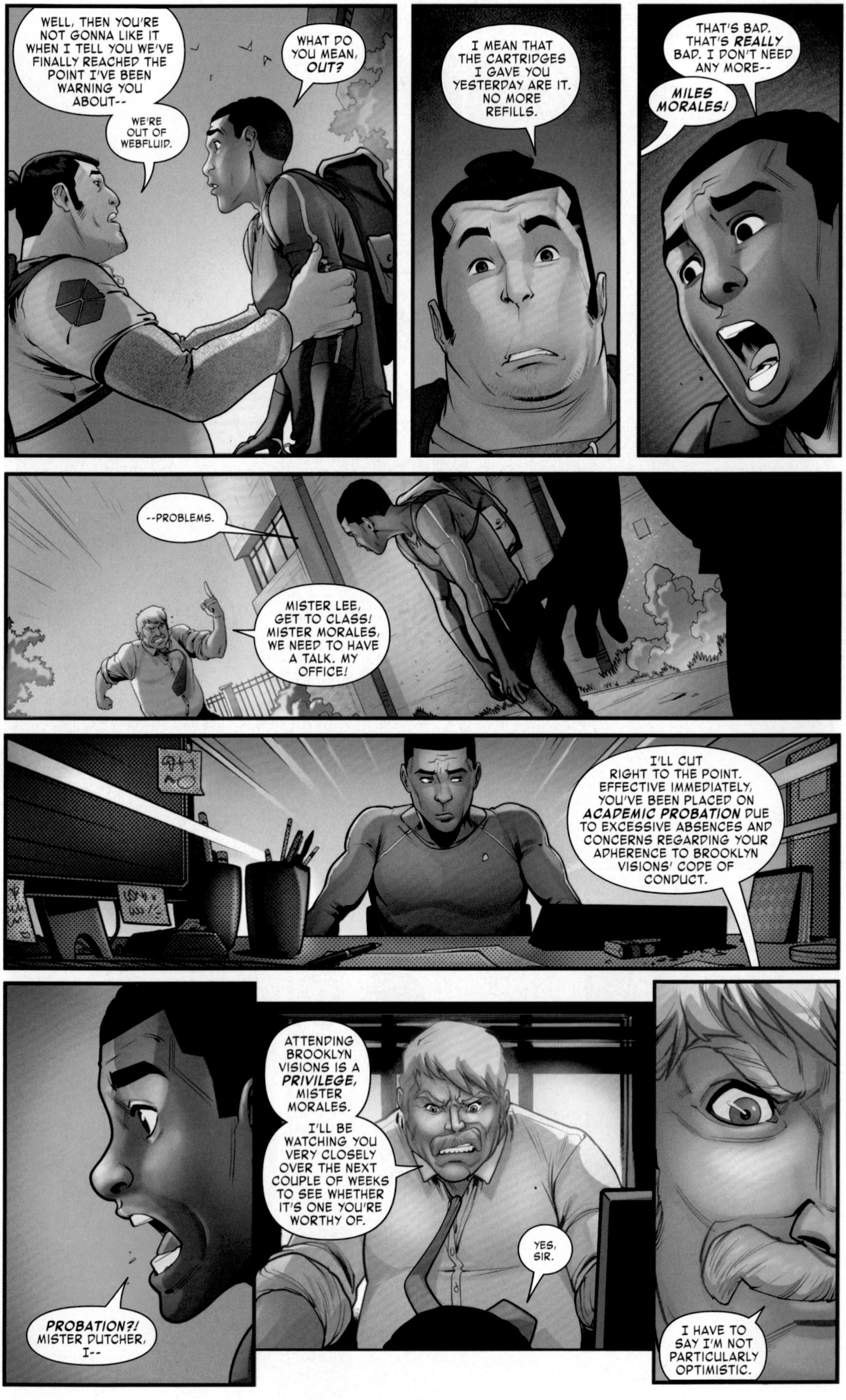
WELL, THEN YOU'RE NOT GONNA LIKE IT WHEN I TELL YOU WE'VE FINALLY REACHED THE POINT I'VE BEEN WARNING YOU ABOUT--
WE'RE OUT OF WEBFLUID.
WHAT DO YOU MEAN, OUT?
I MEAN THAT THE CARTRIDGES I GAVE YOU YESTERDAY ARE IT. NO MORE REFILLS.
THAT'S BAD. THAT'S REALLY BAD. I DON'T NEED ANY MORE--
MILES MORALES!
--PROBLEMS.
MISTER LEE, GET TO CLASS! MISTER MORALES, WE NEED TO HAVE A TALK. MY OFFICE!
I'LL CUT RIGHT TO THE POINT. EFFECTIVE IMMEDIATELY, YOU'VE BEEN PLACED ON ACADEMIC PROBATION DUE TO EXCESSIVE ABSENCES AND CONCERNS REGARDING YOUR ADHERENCE TO BROOKLYN VISIONS' CODE OF CONDUCT.
PROBATION?! MISTER DUTCHER, I--
ATTENDING BROOKLYN VISIONS IS A PRIVILEGE, MISTER MORALES.
I'LL BE WATCHING YOU VERY CLOSELY OVER THE NEXT COUPLE OF WEEKS TO SEE WHETHER IT'S ONE YOU'RE WORTHY OF.
YES, SIR.
I HAVE TO SAY I'M NOT PARTICULARLY OPTIMISTIC.

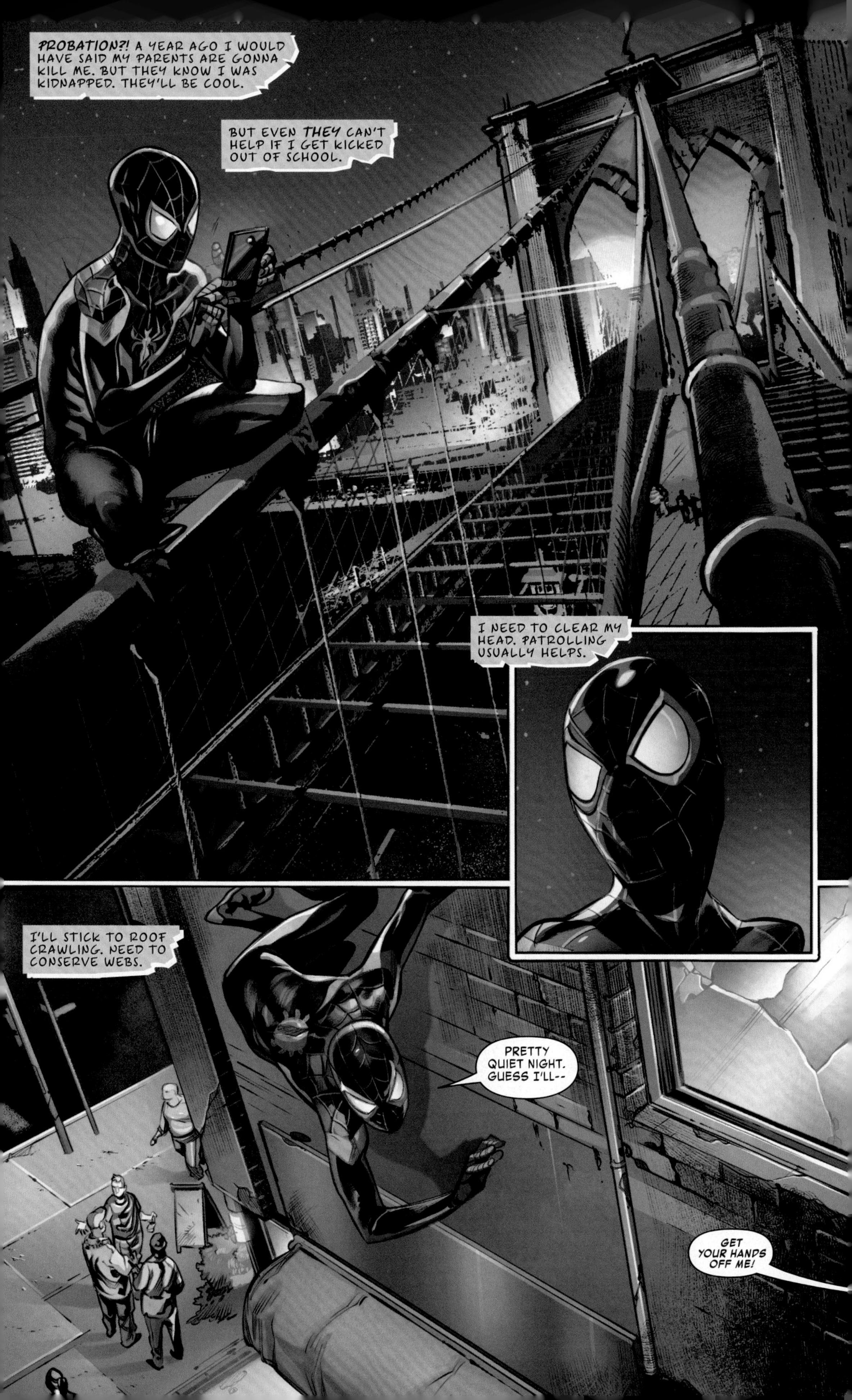
PROBATION?! A YEAR AGO I WOULD HAVE SAID MY PARENTS ARE GONNA KILL ME. BUT THEY KNOW I WAS KIDNAPPED. THEY'LL BE COOL.
BUT EVEN THEY CAN'T HELP IF I GET KICKED OUT OF SCHOOL.
I NEED TO CLEAR MY HEAD. PATROLLING USUALLY HELPS.
I'LL STICK TO ROOF CRAWLING. NEED TO CONSERVE WEBS.
PRETTY QUIET NIGHT. GUESS I'LL--
GET YOUR HANDS OFF ME!

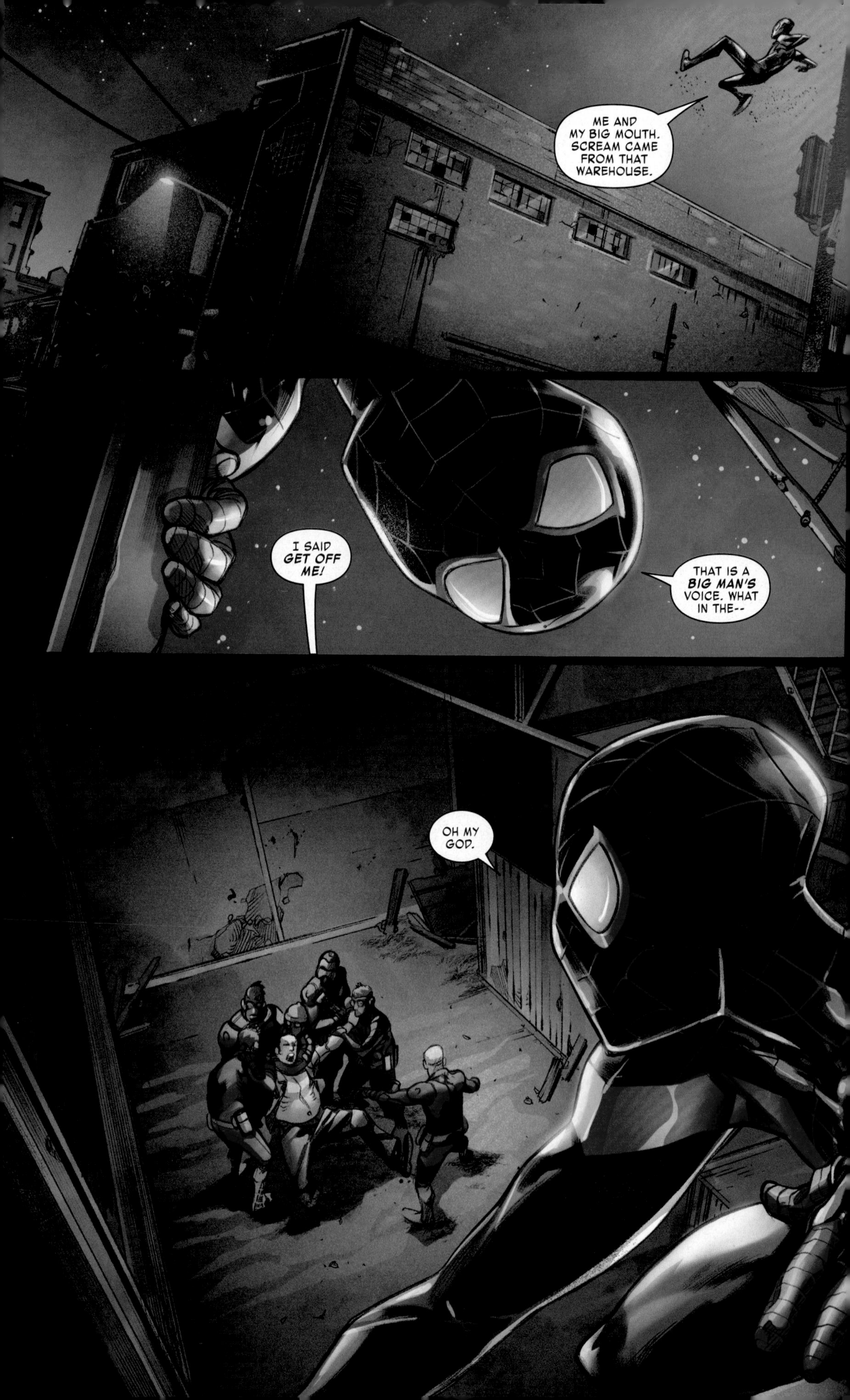
ME AND MY BIG MOUTH. SCREAM CAME FROM THAT WAREHOUSE.
I SAID *GET OFF ME!*
THAT IS A *BIG MAN'S* VOICE. WHAT IN THE--
OH MY GOD.

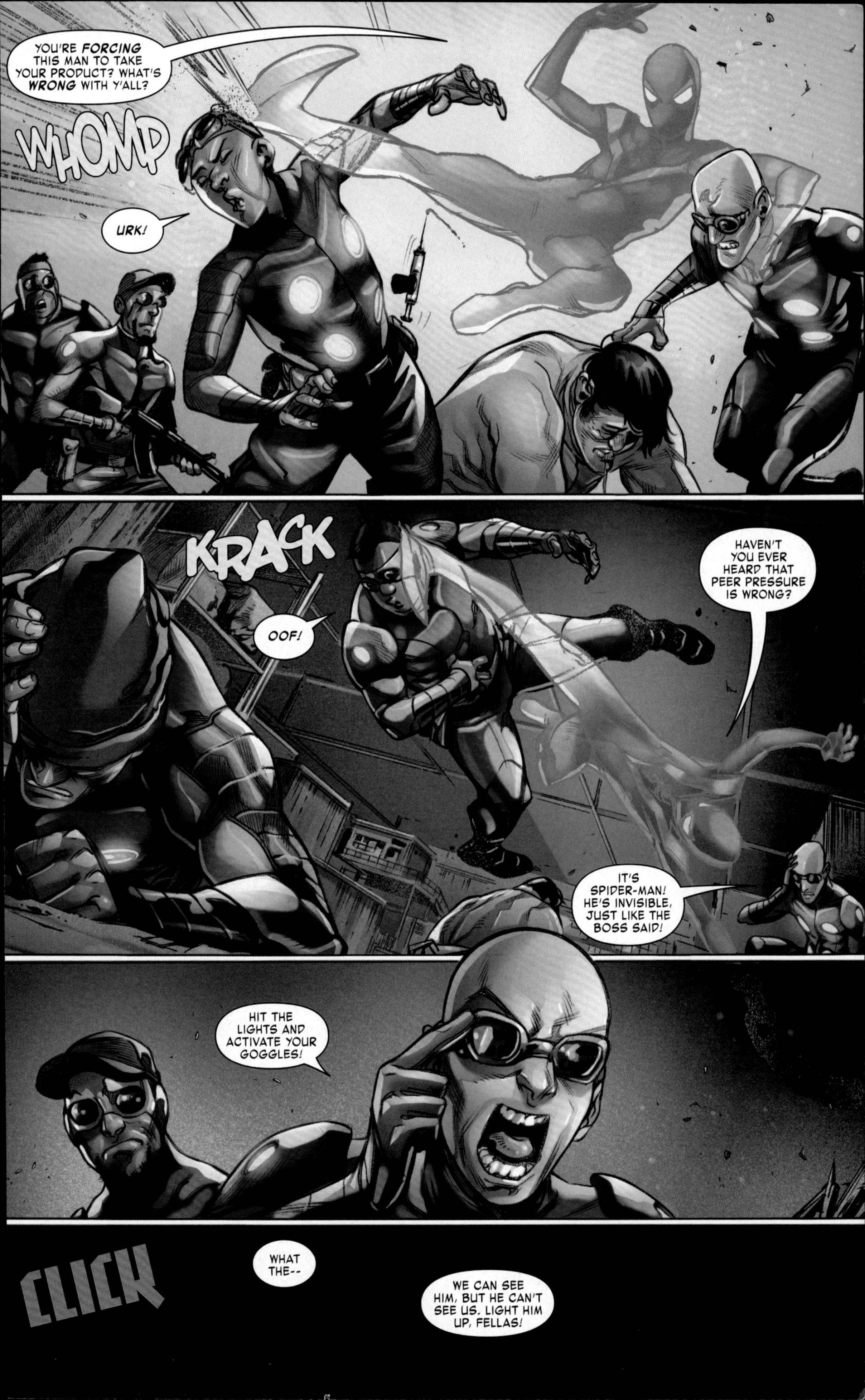
YOU'RE FORCING THIS MAN TO TAKE YOUR PRODUCT? WHAT'S WRONG WITH Y'ALL?
WHOMP
URK!
KRACK
OOF!
HAVEN'T YOU EVER HEARD THAT PEER PRESSURE IS WRONG?
IT'S SPIDER-MAN! HE'S INVISIBLE, JUST LIKE THE BOSS SAID!
HIT THE LIGHTS AND ACTIVATE YOUR GOGGLES!
CLICK
WHAT THE--
WE CAN SEE HIM, BUT HE CAN'T SEE US. LIGHT HIM UP, FELLAS!

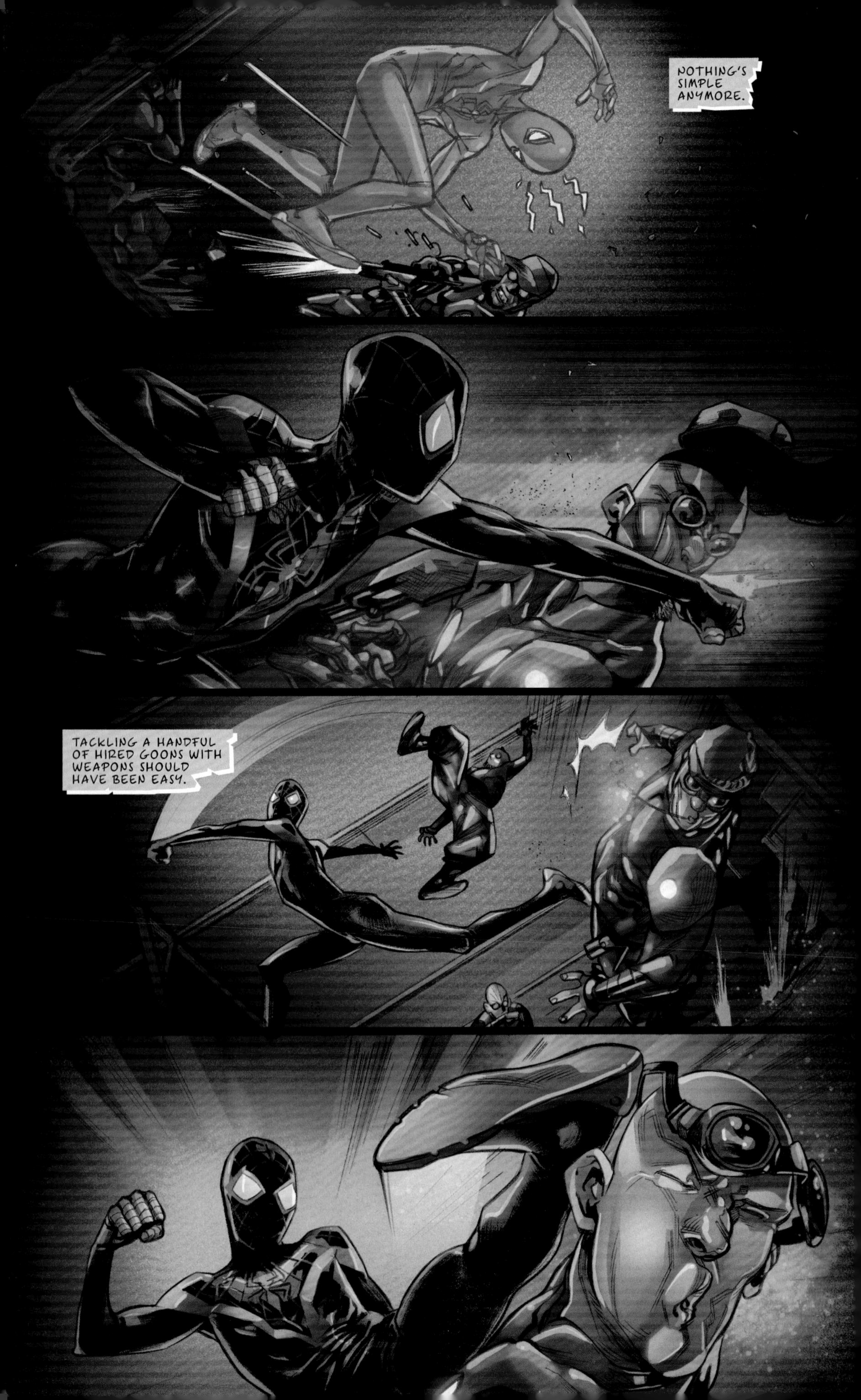
NOTHING'S SIMPLE ANYMORE.
TACKLING A HANDFUL OF HIRED GOONS WITH WEAPONS SHOULD HAVE BEEN EASY.

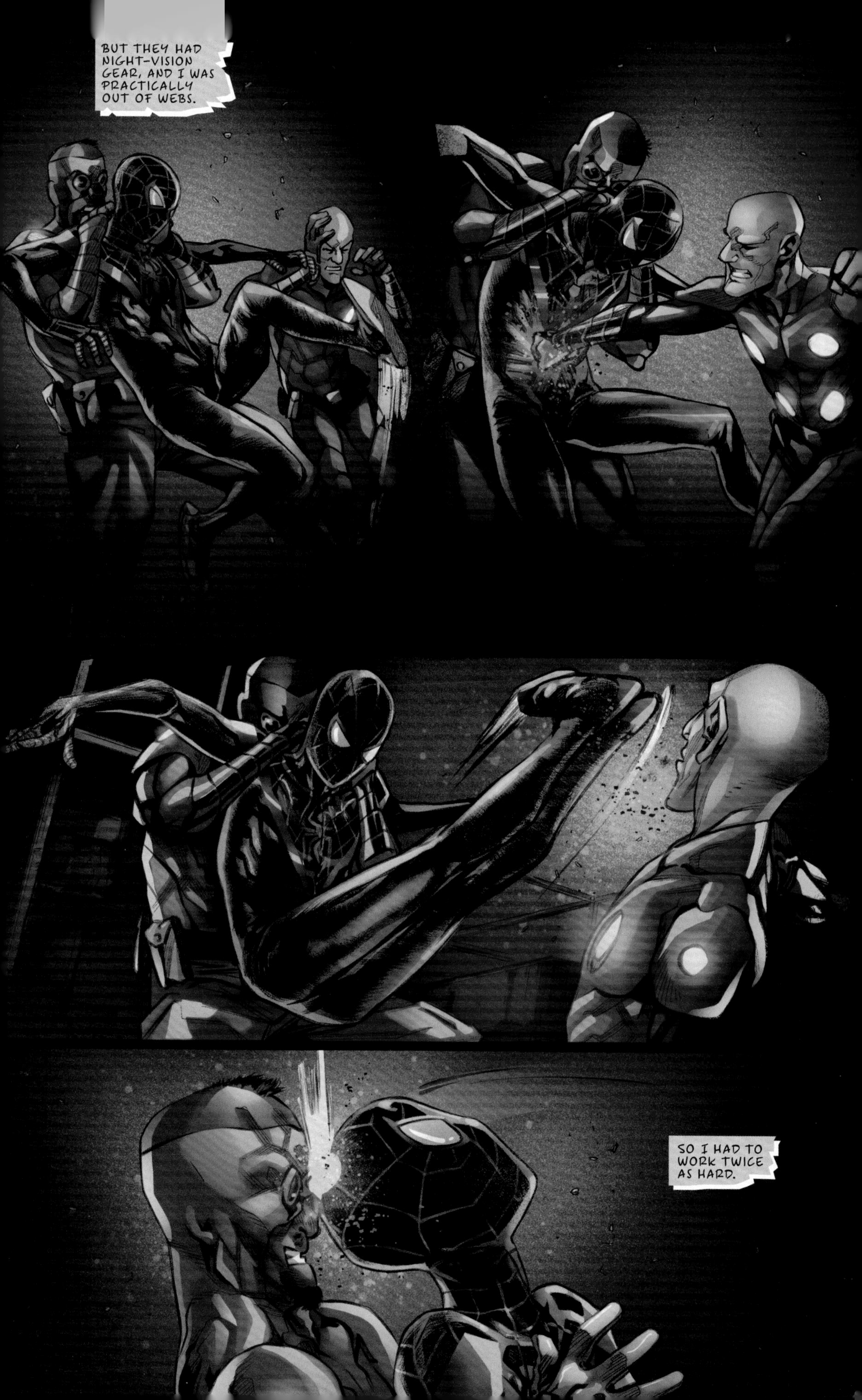
BUT THEY HAD NIGHT-VISION GEAR, AND I WAS PRACTICALLY OUT OF WEBS.
SO I HAD TO WORK TWICE AS HARD.

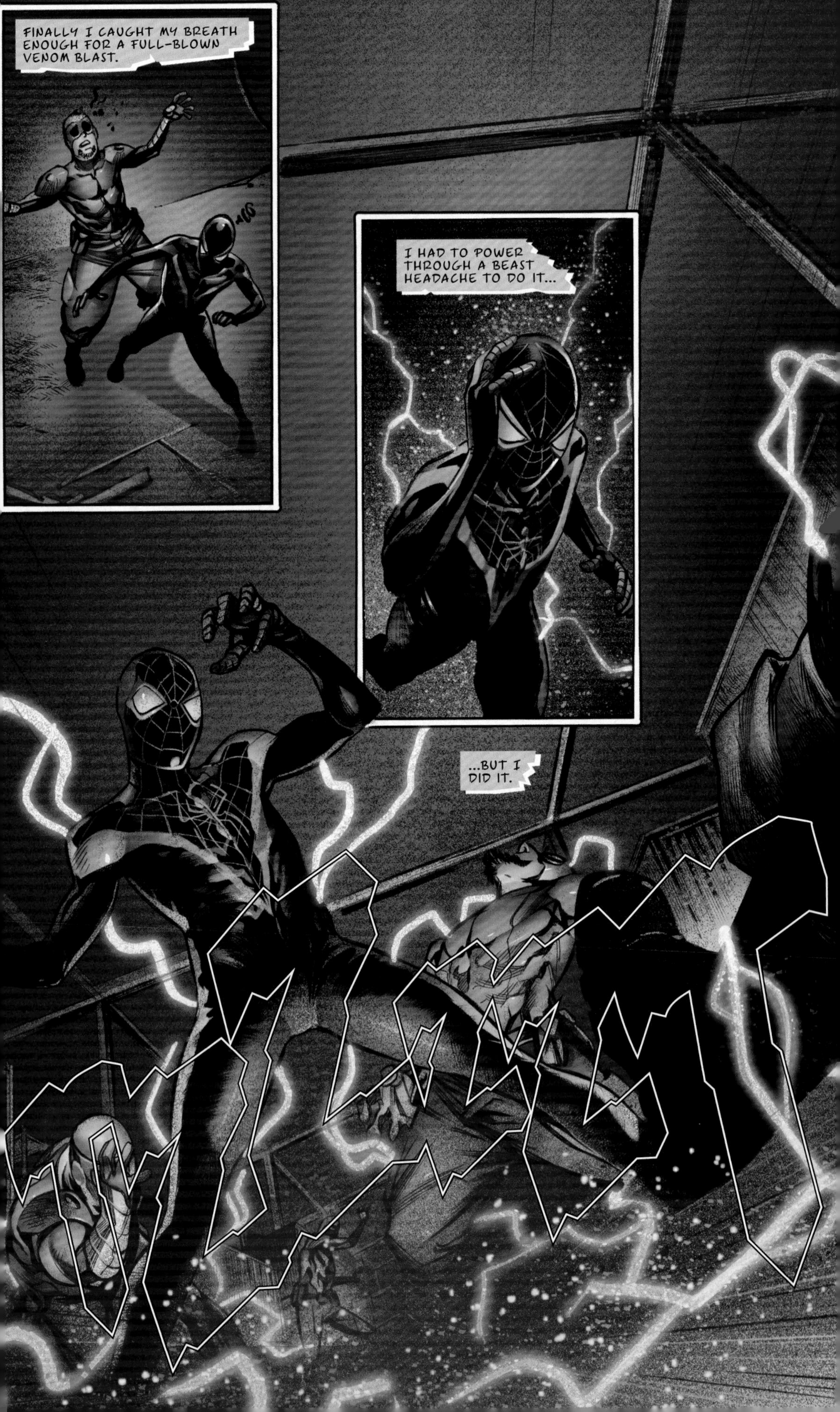

FINALLY I CAUGHT MY BREATH ENOUGH FOR A FULL-BLOWN VENOM BLAST.
I HAD TO POWER THROUGH A BEAST HEADACHE TO DO IT...
...BUT I DID IT.

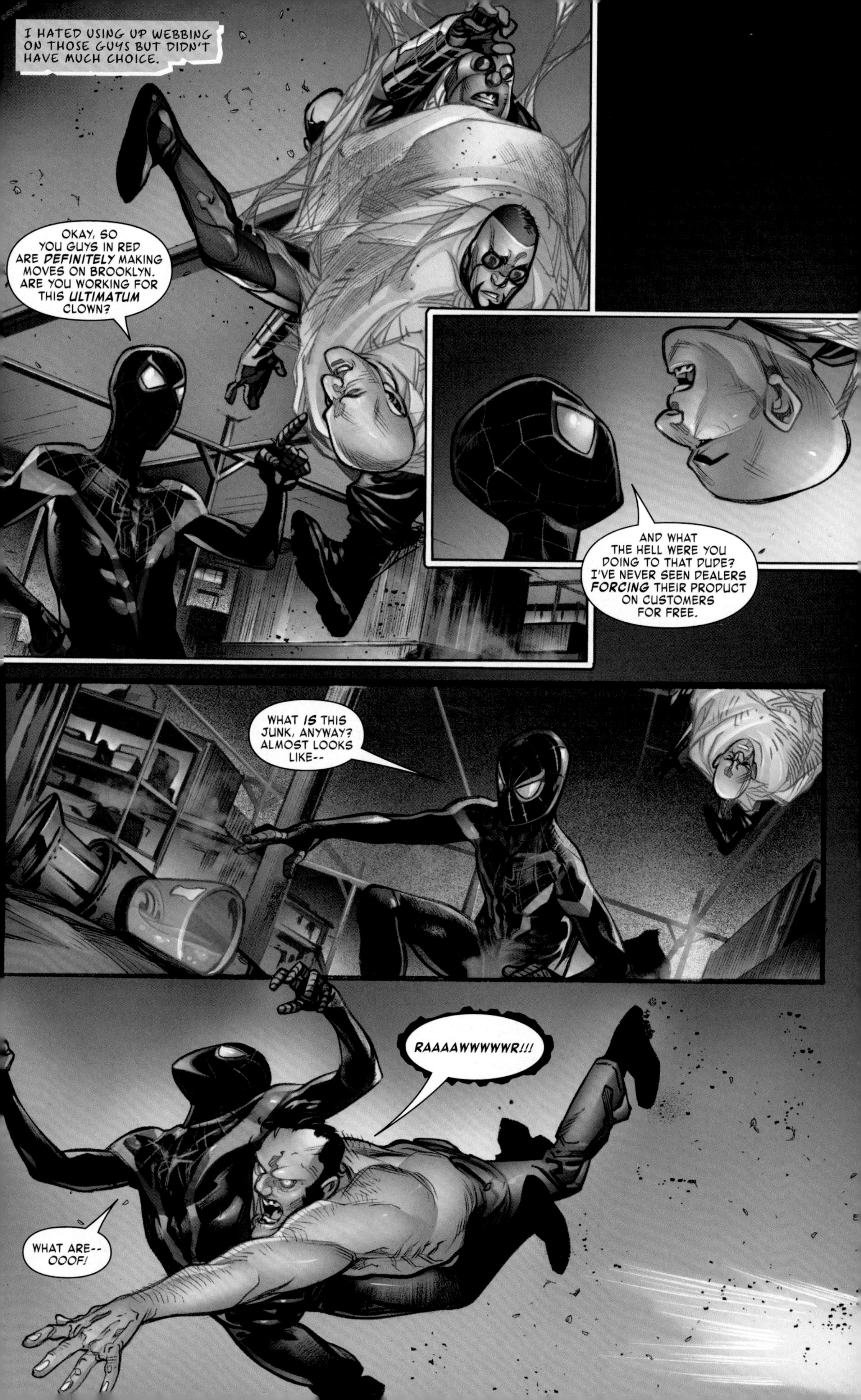

I HATED USING UP WEBBING ON THOSE GUYS BUT DIDN'T HAVE MUCH CHOICE.
OKAY, SO YOU GUYS IN RED ARE DEFINITELY MAKING MOVES ON BROOKLYN. ARE YOU WORKING FOR THIS ULTIMATUM CLOWN?
AND WHAT THE HELL WERE YOU DOING TO THAT DUDE? I'VE NEVER SEEN DEALERS FORCING THEIR PRODUCT ON CUSTOMERS FOR FREE.
WHAT IS THIS JUNK, ANYWAY? ALMOST LOOKS LIKE--
RAAAAWWWWWR!!!
WHAT ARE-- OOOF!

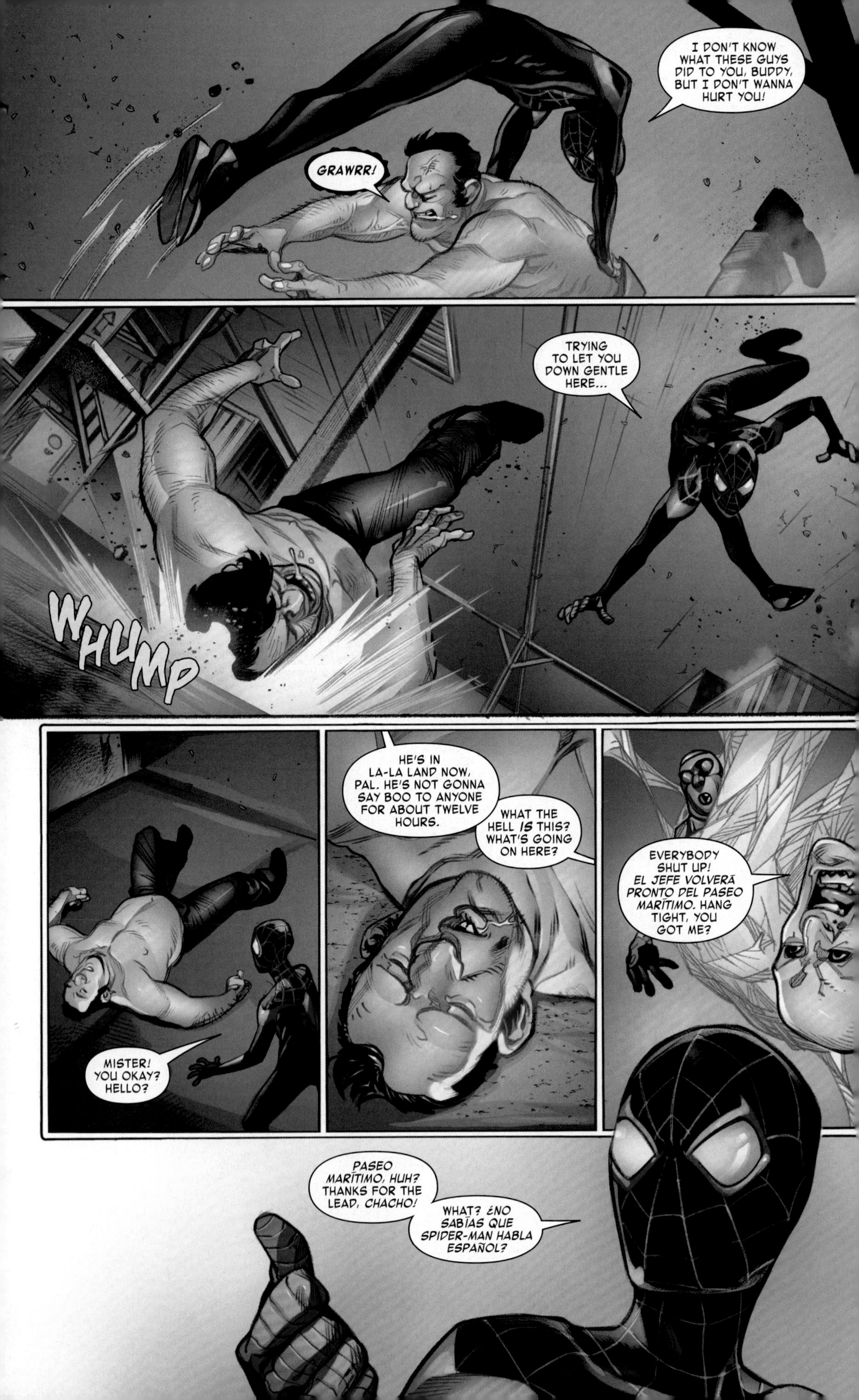
I DON'T KNOW WHAT THESE GUYS DID TO YOU, BUDDY, BUT I DON'T WANNA HURT YOU!
GRAWRR!
TRYING TO LET YOU DOWN GENTLE HERE...
WHUMP
MISTER! YOU OKAY? HELLO?
HE'S IN LA-LA LAND NOW, PAL. HE'S NOT GONNA SAY BOO TO ANYONE FOR ABOUT TWELVE HOURS.
WHAT THE HELL *IS* THIS? WHAT'S GOING ON HERE?
EVERYBODY SHUT UP! *EL JEFE VOLVERÁ PRONTO DEL PASEO MARÍTIMO.* HANG TIGHT, YOU GOT ME?
PASEO MARÍTIMO, HUH? THANKS FOR THE LEAD, CHACHO!
WHAT? *¿NO SABÍAS QUE SPIDER-MAN HABLA ESPAÑOL?*

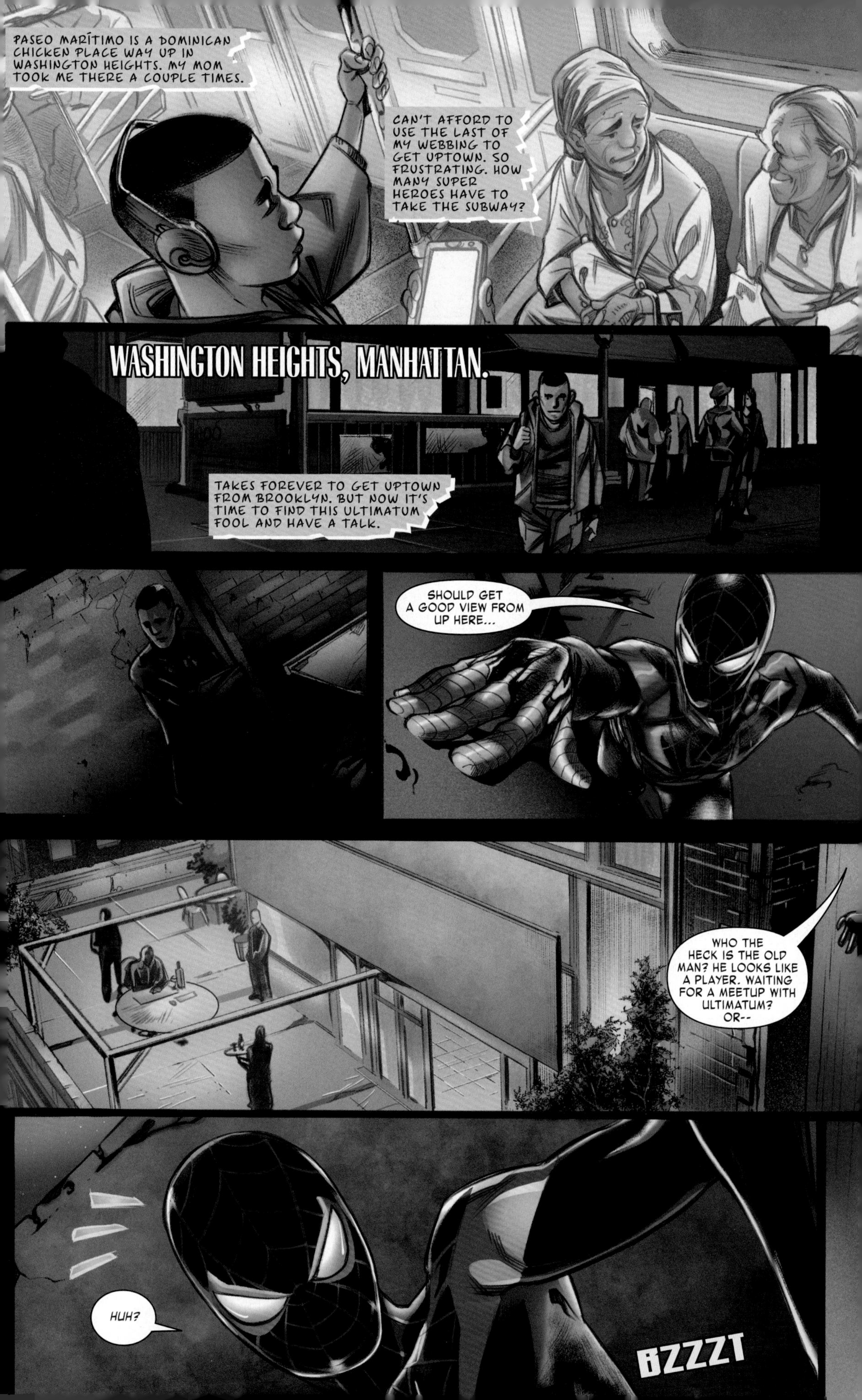
PASEO MARÍTIMO IS A DOMINICAN CHICKEN PLACE WAY UP IN WASHINGTON HEIGHTS. MY MOM TOOK ME THERE A COUPLE TIMES.
CAN'T AFFORD TO USE THE LAST OF MY WEBBING TO GET UPTOWN. SO FRUSTRATING. HOW MANY SUPER HEROES HAVE TO TAKE THE SUBWAY?
WASHINGTON HEIGHTS, MANHATTAN.
TAKES FOREVER TO GET UPTOWN FROM BROOKLYN. BUT NOW IT'S TIME TO FIND THIS ULTIMATUM FOOL AND HAVE A TALK.
SHOULD GET A GOOD VIEW FROM UP HERE...
WHO THE HECK IS THE OLD MAN? HE LOOKS LIKE A PLAYER. WAITING FOR A MEETUP WITH ULTIMATUM? OR--
HUH?
BZZZT

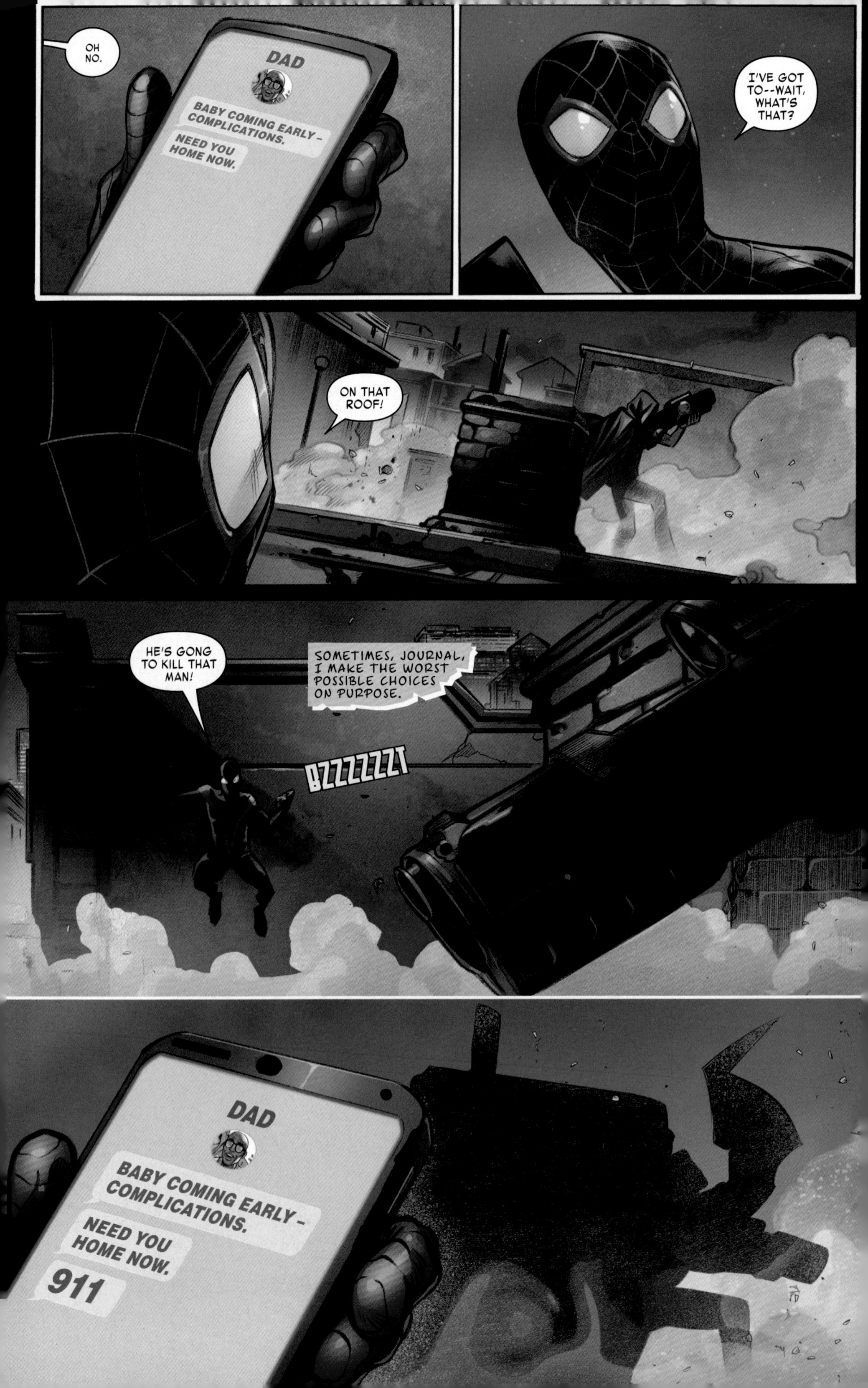
OH NO.
DAD
BABY COMING EARLY – COMPLICATIONS.
NEED YOU HOME NOW.
I'VE GOT TO--WAIT, WHAT'S THAT?
ON THAT ROOF!
HE'S GONG TO KILL THAT MAN!
SOMETIMES, JOURNAL, I MAKE THE WORST POSSIBLE CHOICES ON PURPOSE.
BZZZZZZT
DAD
BABY COMING EARLY – COMPLICATIONS.
NEED YOU HOME NOW.
911

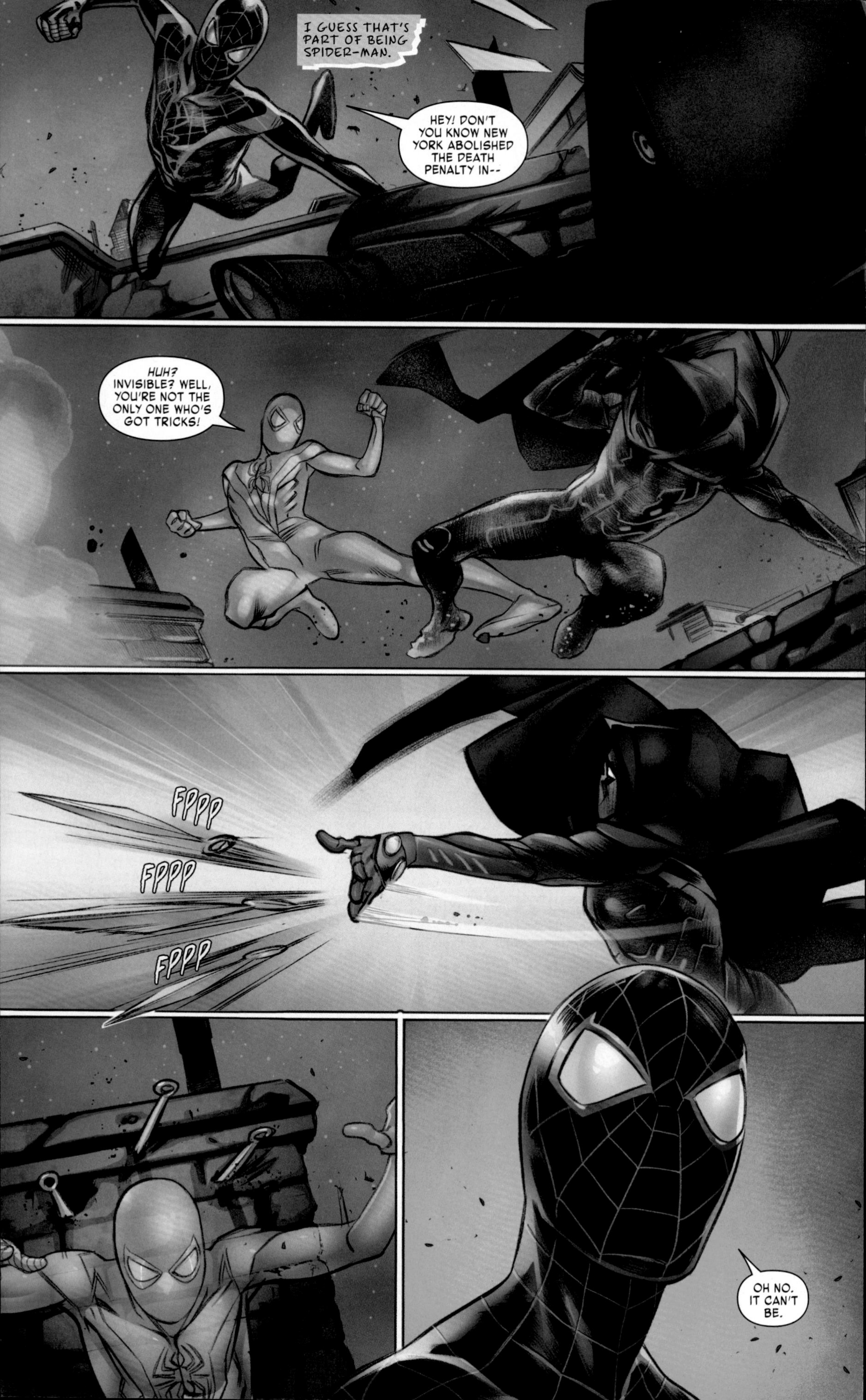
I GUESS THAT'S PART OF BEING SPIDER-MAN.
HEY! DON'T YOU KNOW NEW YORK ABOLISHED THE DEATH PENALTY IN--
HUH? INVISIBLE? WELL, YOU'RE NOT THE ONLY ONE WHO'S GOT TRICKS!
FPPP
FPPP
FPPP
OH NO. IT CAN'T BE.

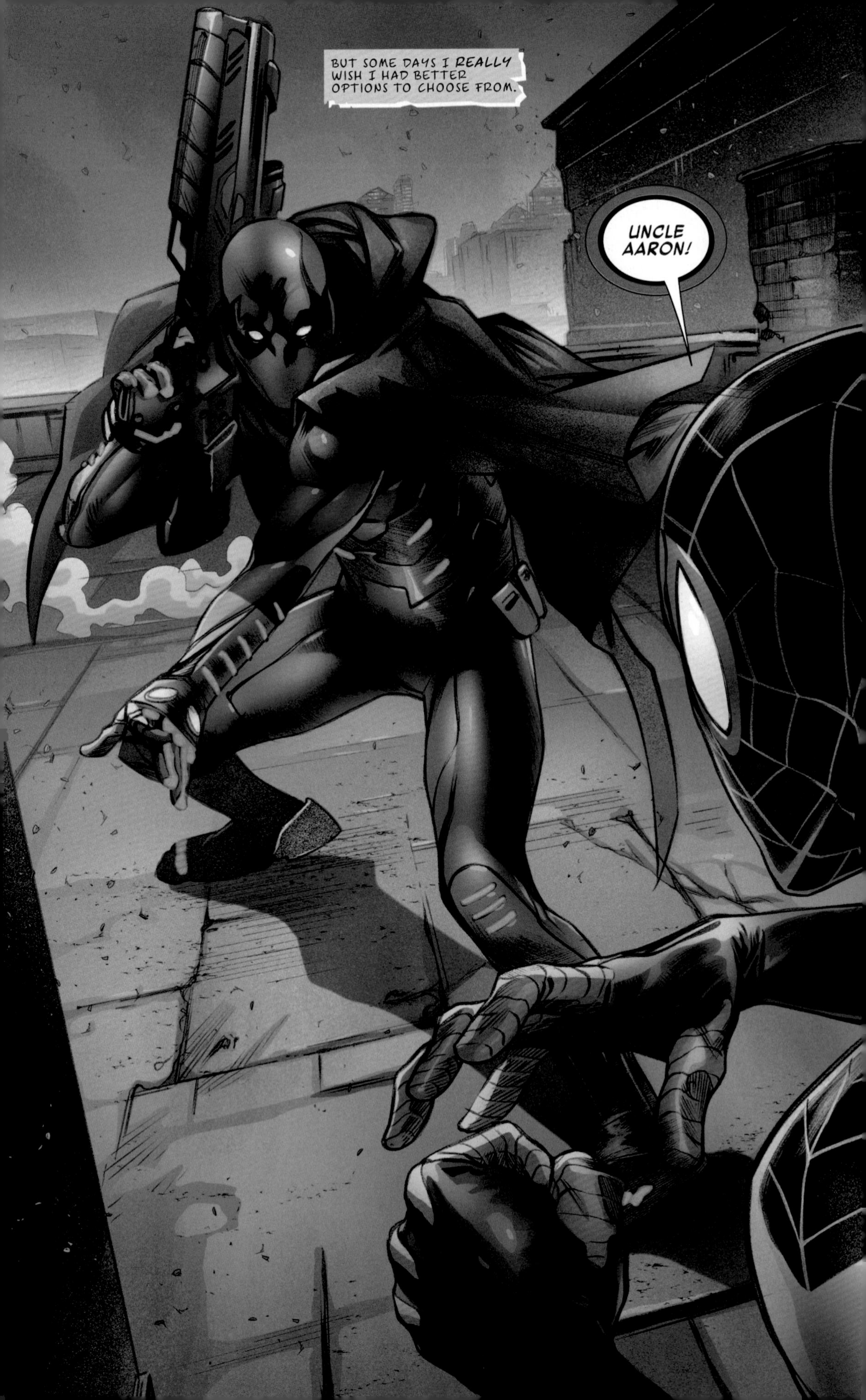
BUT SOME DAYS I REALLY WISH I HAD BETTER OPTIONS TO CHOOSE FROM.
UNCLE AARON!

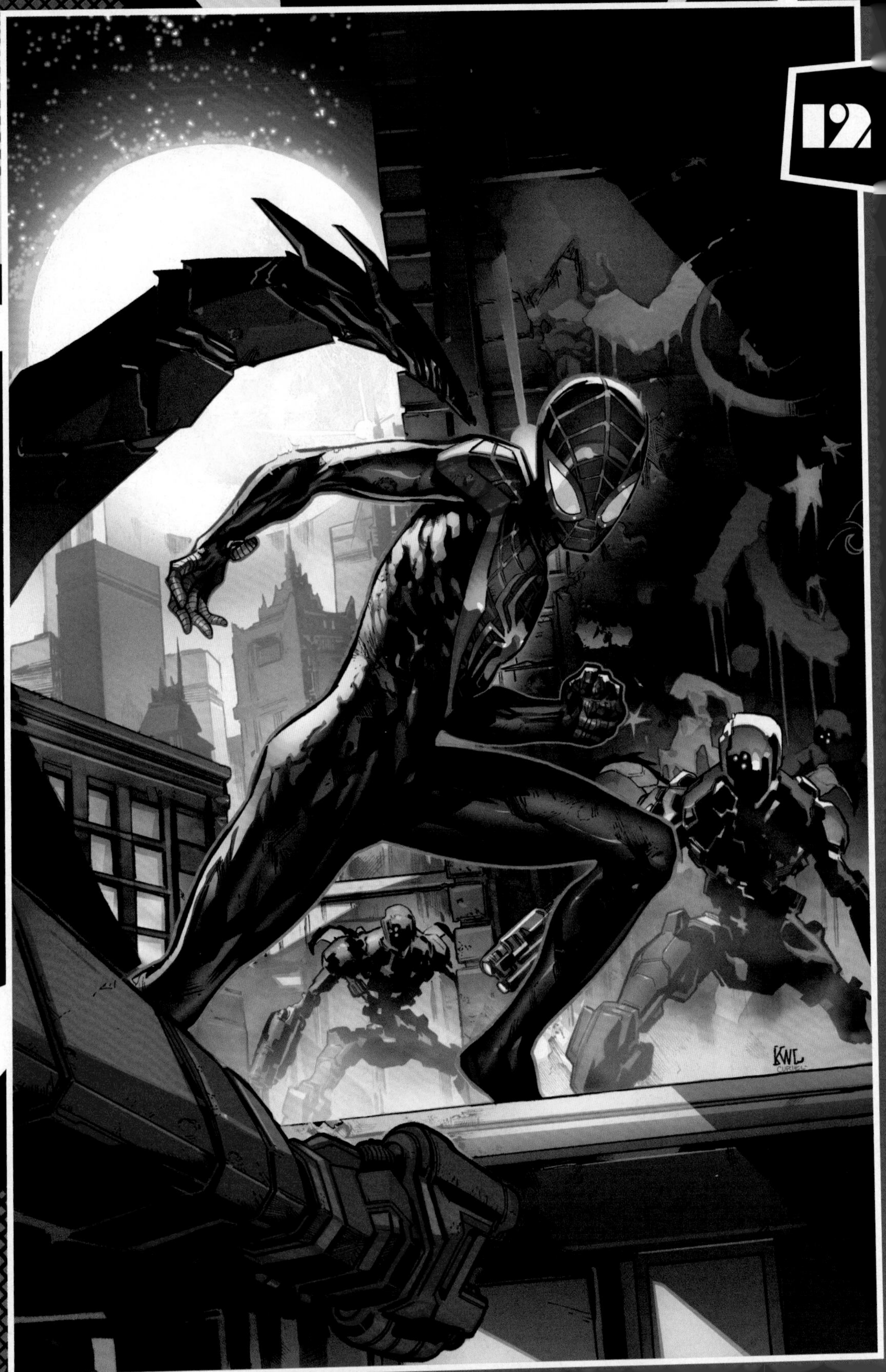
12

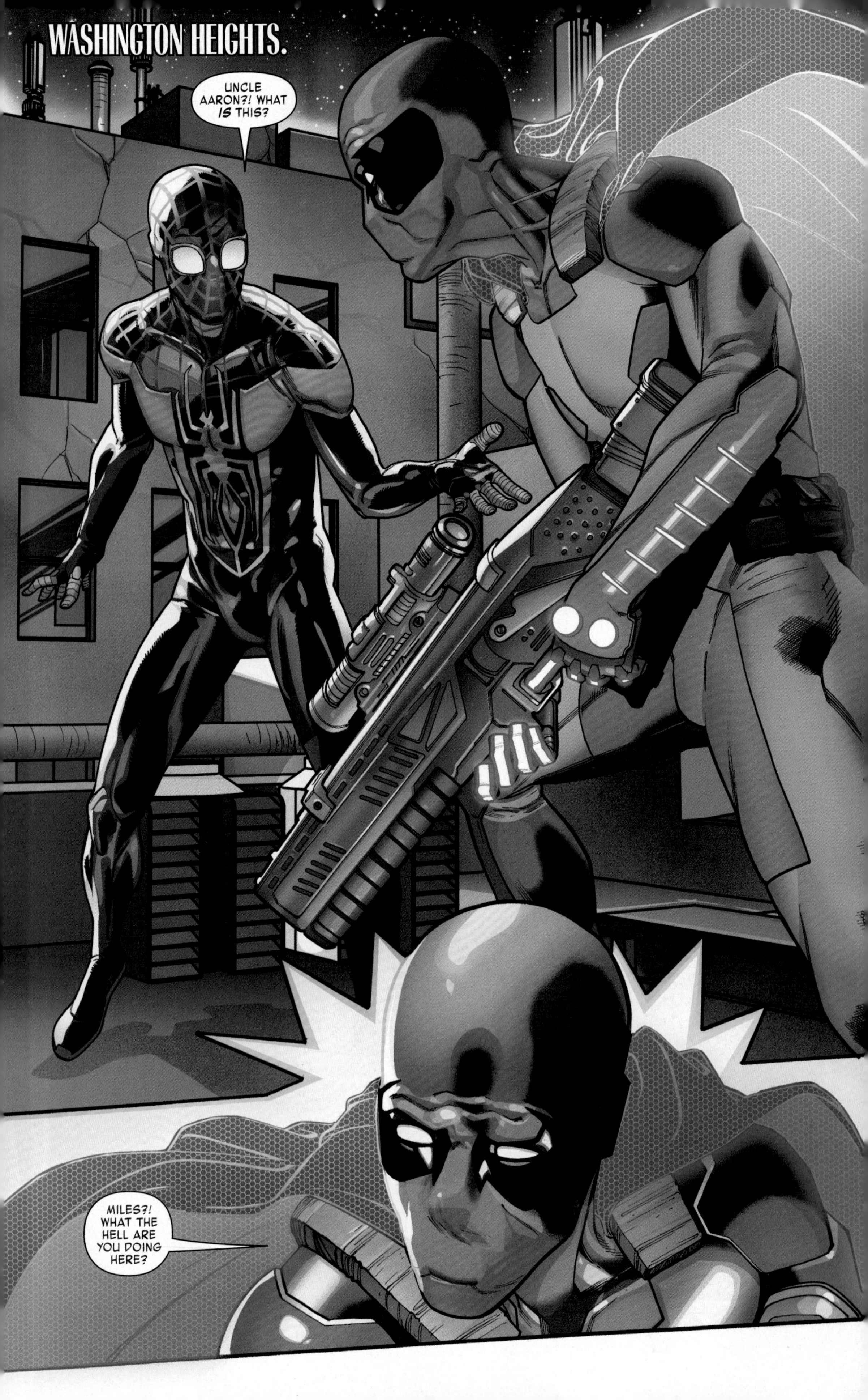
WASHINGTON HEIGHTS.
UNCLE AARON?! WHAT IS THIS?
MILES?! WHAT THE HELL ARE YOU DOING HERE?

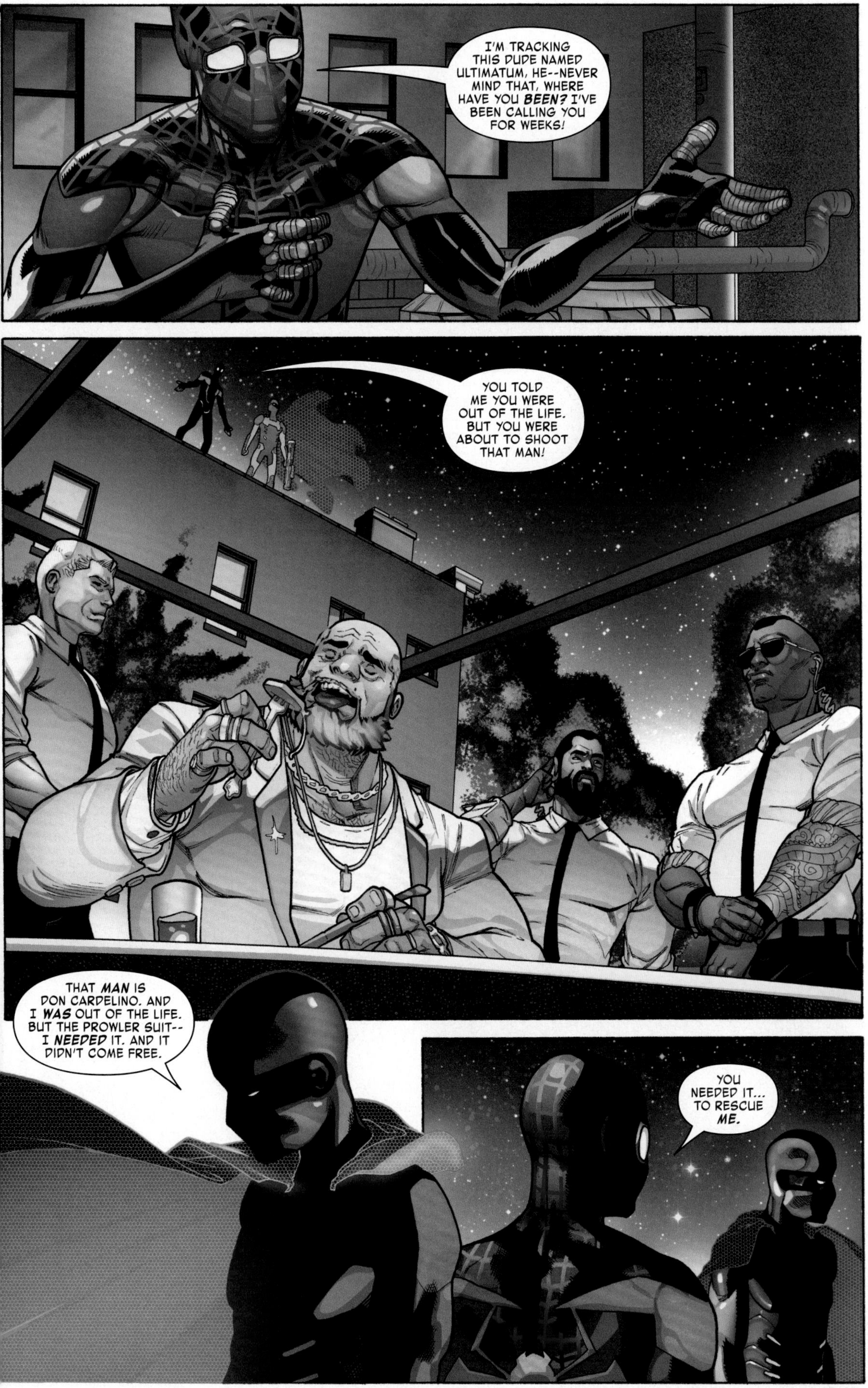
I'M TRACKING THIS DUDE NAMED ULTIMATUM, HE--NEVER MIND THAT, WHERE HAVE YOU BEEN? I'VE BEEN CALLING YOU FOR WEEKS!
YOU TOLD ME YOU WERE OUT OF THE LIFE. BUT YOU WERE ABOUT TO SHOOT THAT MAN!
THAT MAN IS DON CARDELINO. AND I WAS OUT OF THE LIFE. BUT THE PROWLER SUIT-- I NEEDED IT. AND IT DIDN'T COME FREE.
YOU NEEDED IT... TO RESCUE ME.

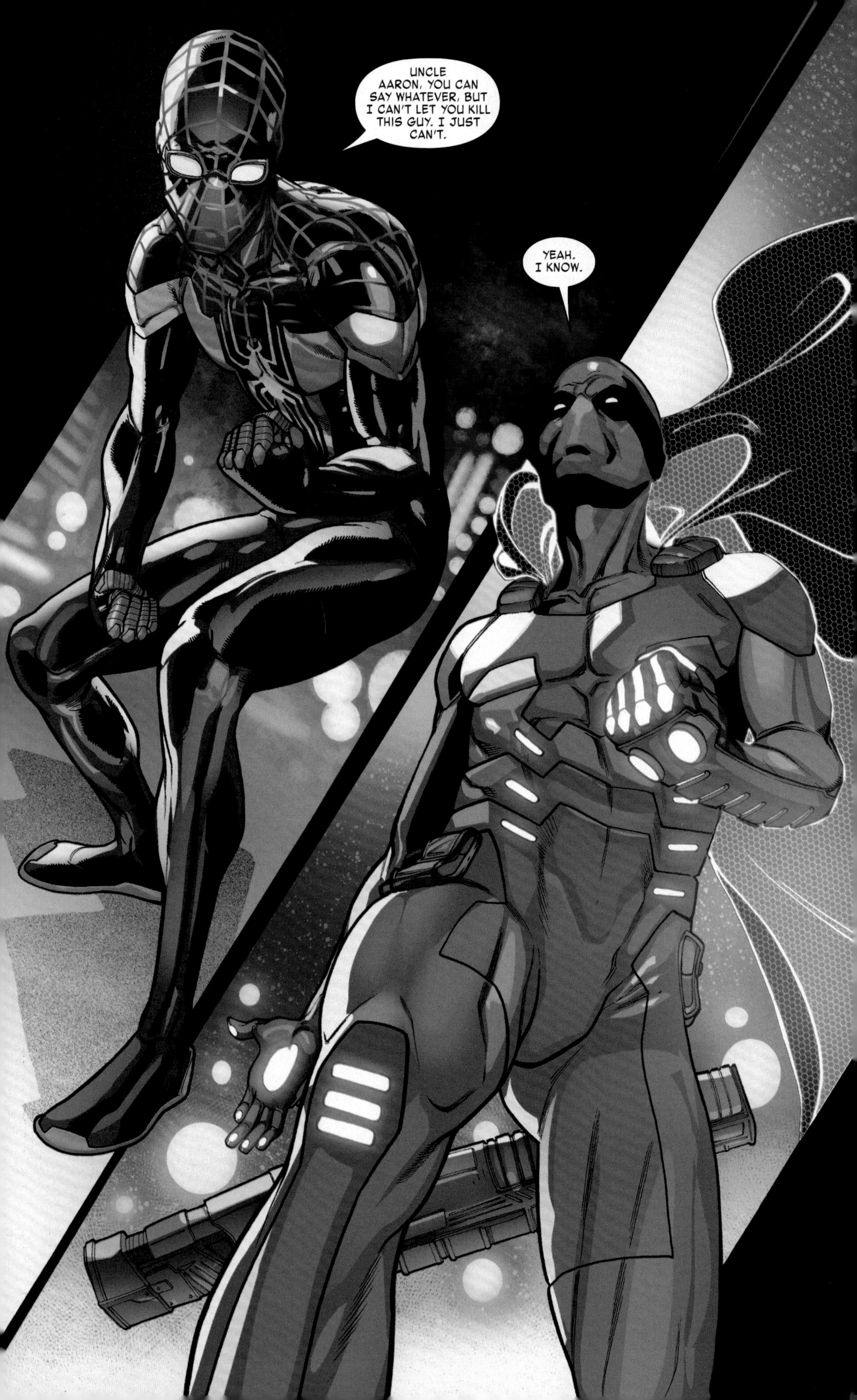
UNCLE AARON, YOU CAN SAY WHATEVER, BUT I CAN'T LET YOU KILL THIS GUY. I JUST CAN'T.
YEAH. I KNOW.

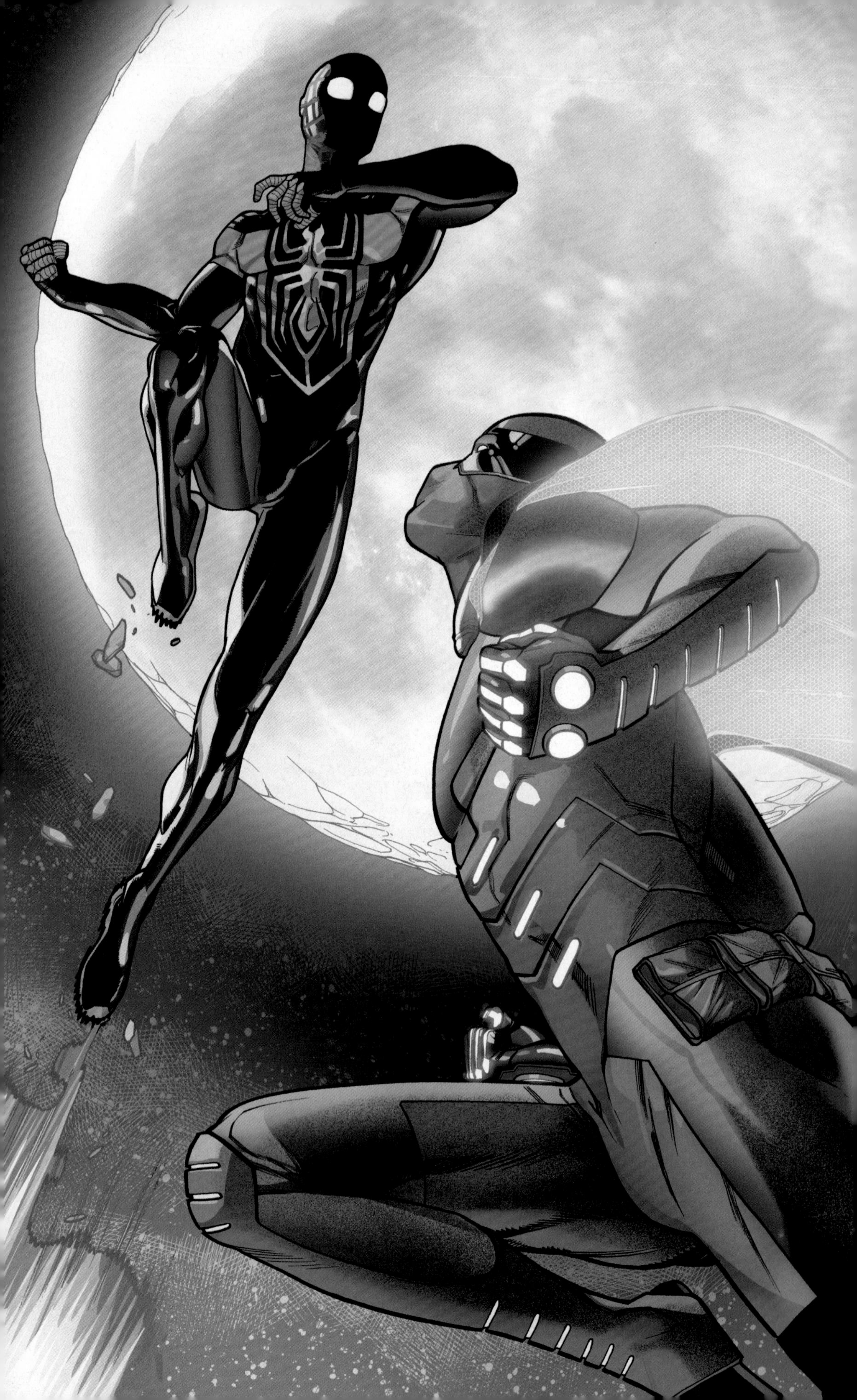

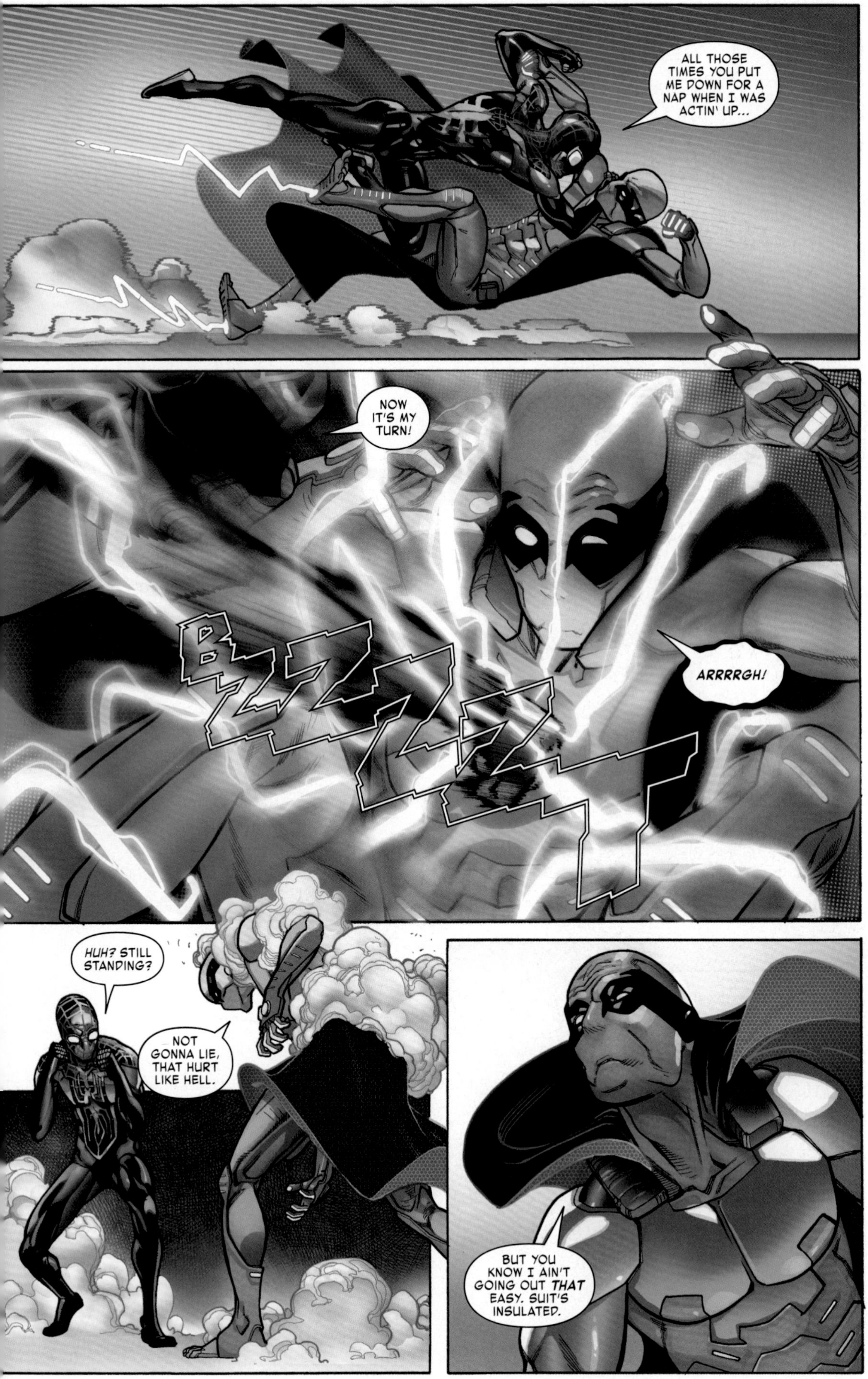
ALL THOSE TIMES YOU PUT ME DOWN FOR A NAP WHEN I WAS ACTIN' UP...
NOW IT'S MY TURN!
BZZZZT
ARRRRGH!
HUH? STILL STANDING?
NOT GONNA LIE, THAT HURT LIKE HELL.
BUT YOU KNOW I AIN'T GOING OUT *THAT* EASY. SUIT'S INSULATED.

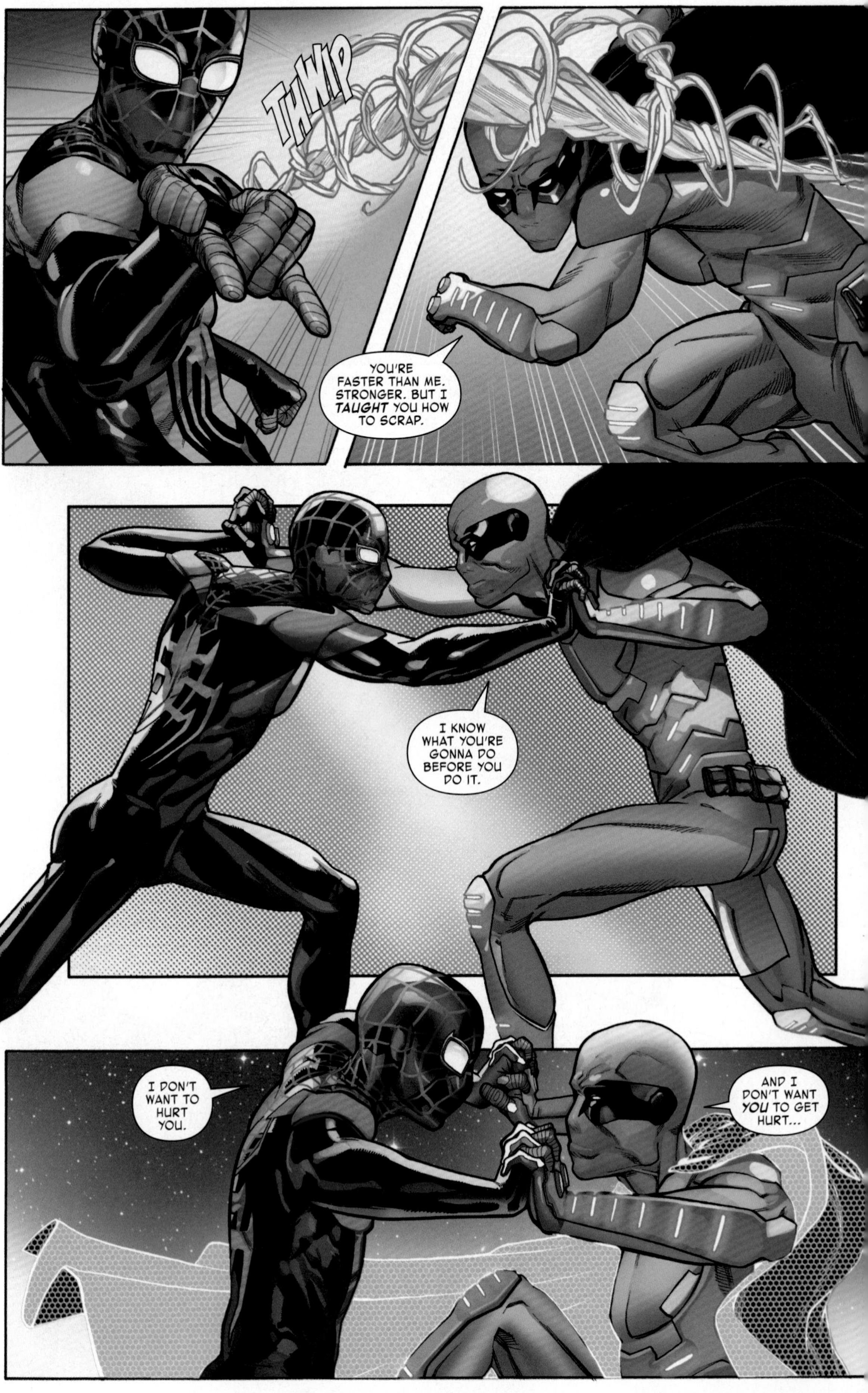
THWIP
YOU'RE FASTER THAN ME. STRONGER. BUT I TAUGHT YOU HOW TO SCRAP.
I KNOW WHAT YOU'RE GONNA DO BEFORE YOU DO IT.
I DON'T WANT TO HURT YOU.
AND I DON'T WANT YOU TO GET HURT...

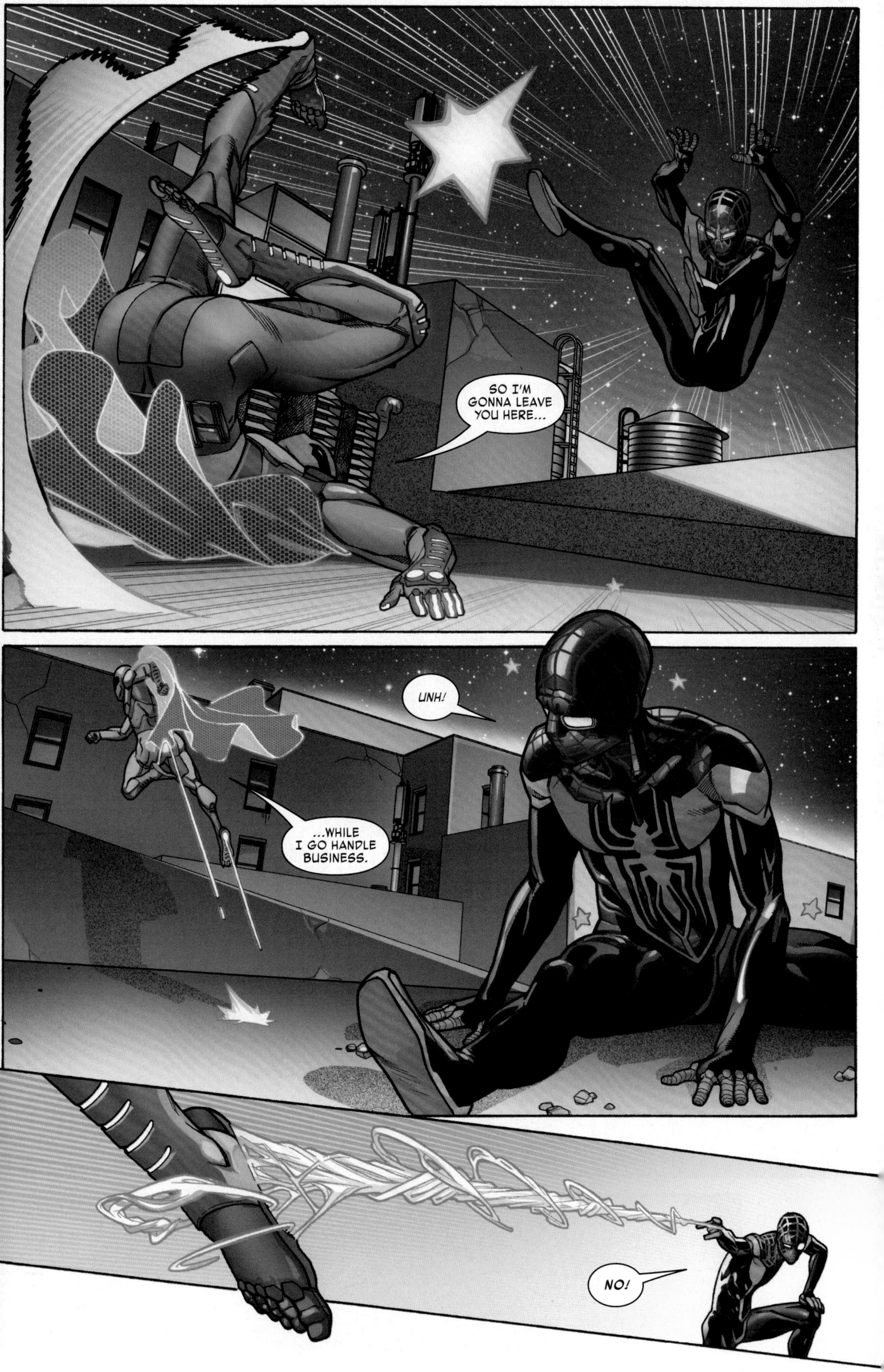
SO I'M GONNA LEAVE YOU HERE...
UNH!
...WHILE I GO HANDLE BUSINESS.
NO!

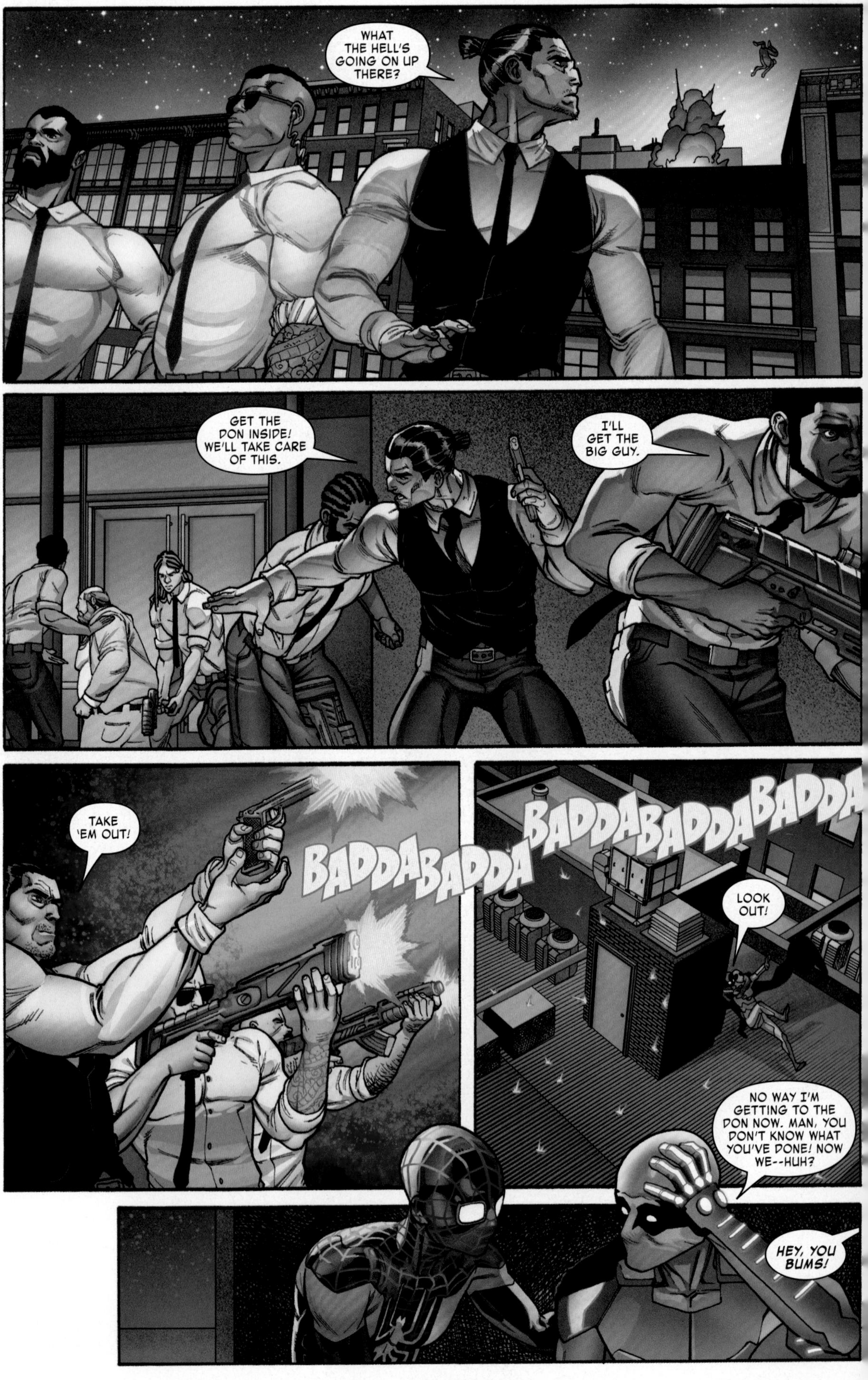
WHAT THE HELL'S GOING ON UP THERE?
GET THE DON INSIDE! WE'LL TAKE CARE OF THIS.
I'LL GET THE BIG GUY.
TAKE 'EM OUT!
BADDABADDA
BADDABADDABADDA
LOOK OUT!
NO WAY I'M GETTING TO THE DON NOW. MAN, YOU DON'T KNOW WHAT YOU'VE DONE! NOW WE--HUH?
HEY, YOU BUMS!

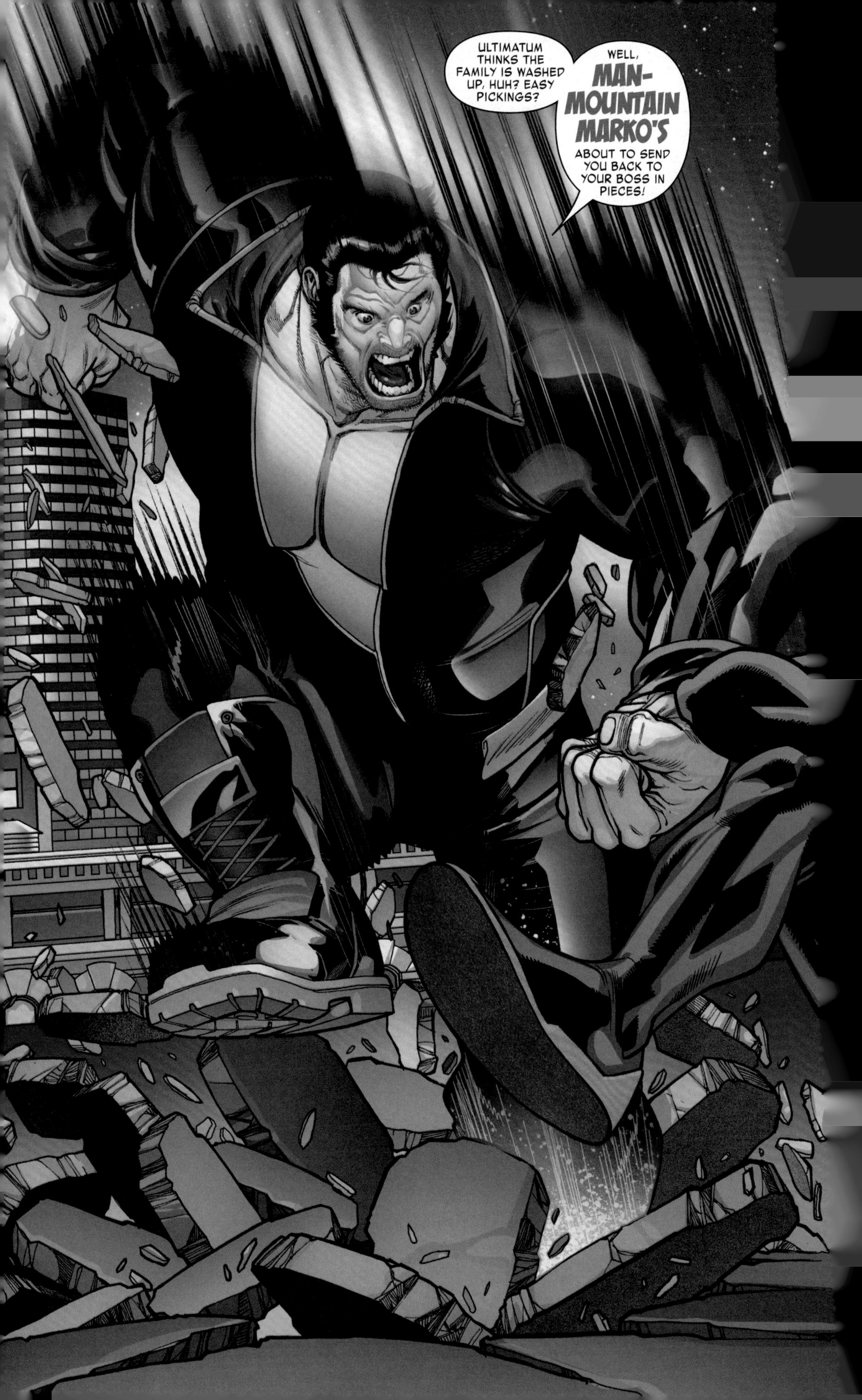
ULTIMATUM THINKS THE FAMILY IS WASHED UP, HUH? EASY PICKINGS?
WELL, MAN-MOUNTAIN MARKO'S ABOUT TO SEND YOU BACK TO YOUR BOSS IN PIECES!

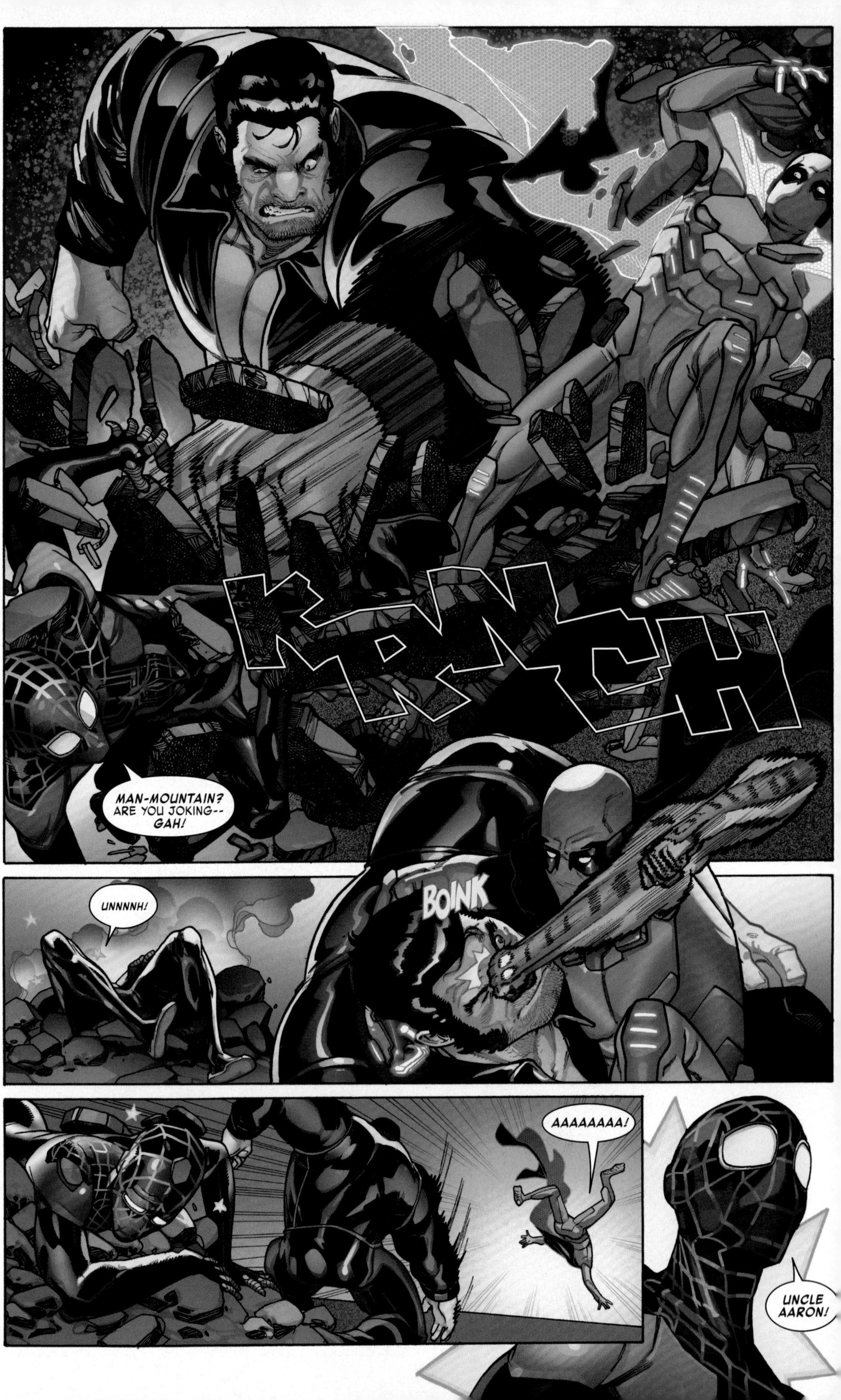
KRNCH
MAN-MOUNTAIN? ARE YOU JOKING-- GAH!
BOINK
UNNNNH!
AAAAAAAA!
UNCLE AARON!

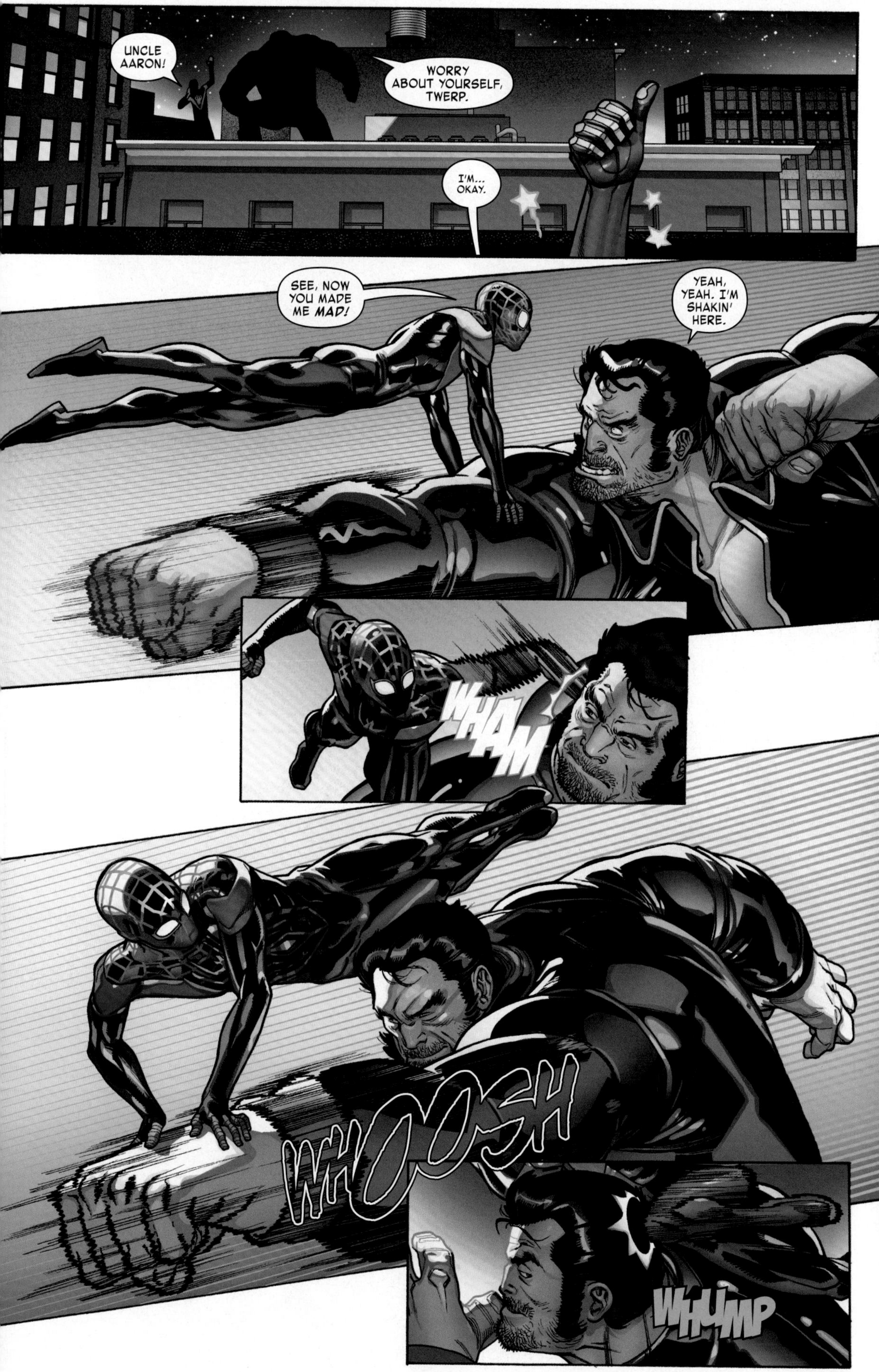
UNCLE AARON!
WORRY ABOUT YOURSELF, TWERP.
I'M... OKAY.
SEE, NOW YOU MADE ME MAD!
YEAH, YEAH. I'M SHAKIN' HERE.
WHAM
WHOOSH
WHUMP

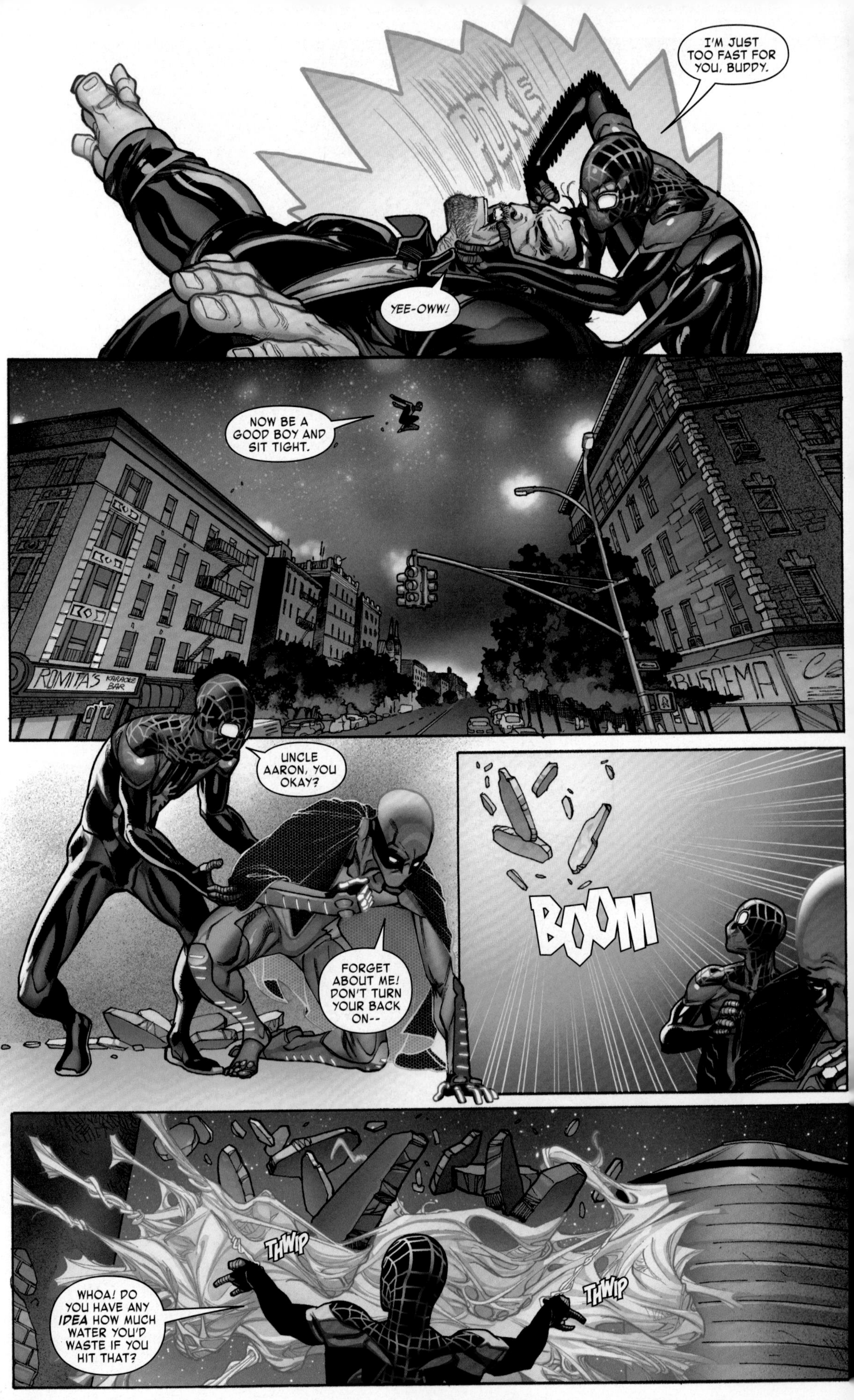

I'M JUST TOO FAST FOR YOU, BUDDY.
YEE-OWW!
NOW BE A GOOD BOY AND SIT TIGHT.
ROMITA'S KARAOKE BAR
BUSCEMA
UNCLE AARON, YOU OKAY?
FORGET ABOUT ME! DON'T TURN YOUR BACK ON--
BOOM
THWIP
THWIP
WHOA! DO YOU HAVE ANY *IDEA* HOW MUCH WATER YOU'D WASTE IF YOU HIT THAT?

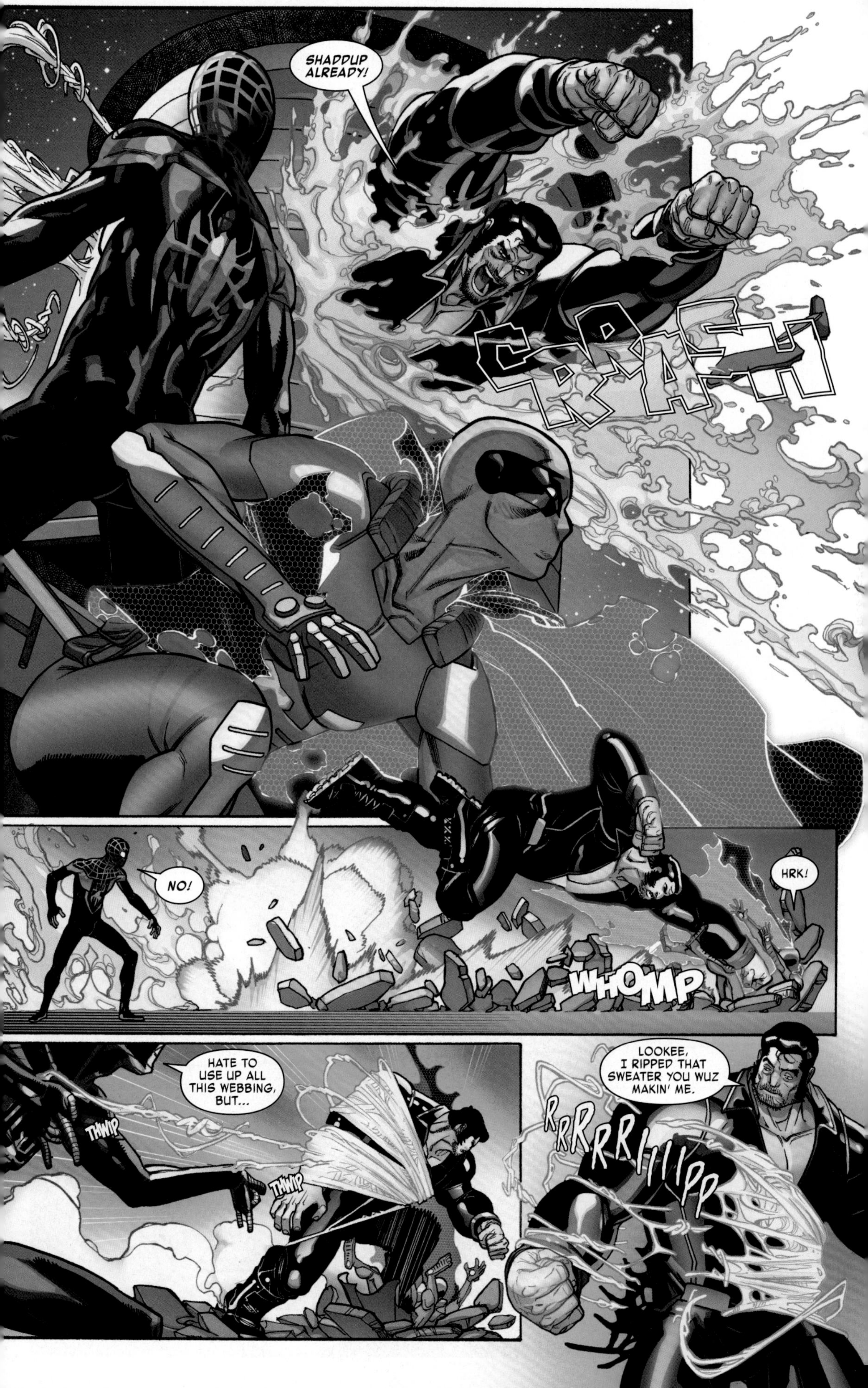
SHADDUP ALREADY!
CRASH
NO!
HRK!
WHOMP
HATE TO USE UP ALL THIS WEBBING, BUT...
THWIP
THWIP
LOOKEE, I RIPPED THAT SWEATER YOU WUZ MAKIN' ME.
RRRRRIIIIPP

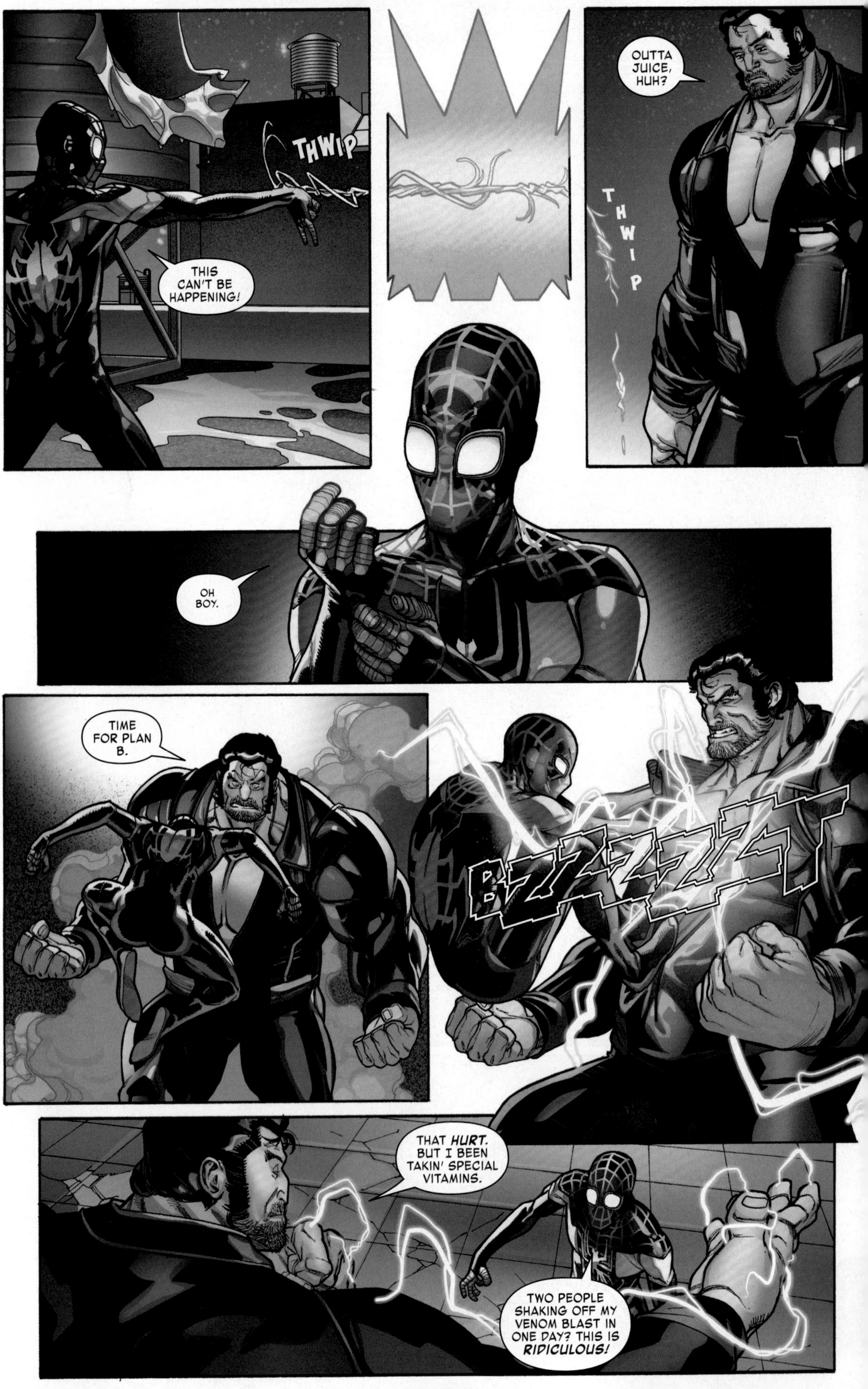

THWIP
THIS CAN'T BE HAPPENING!
OUTTA JUICE, HUH?
THWIP
OH BOY.
TIME FOR PLAN B.
BZZZZZT
THAT *HURT.* BUT I BEEN TAKIN' SPECIAL VITAMINS.
TWO PEOPLE SHAKING OFF MY VENOM BLAST IN ONE DAY? THIS IS *RIDICULOUS!*

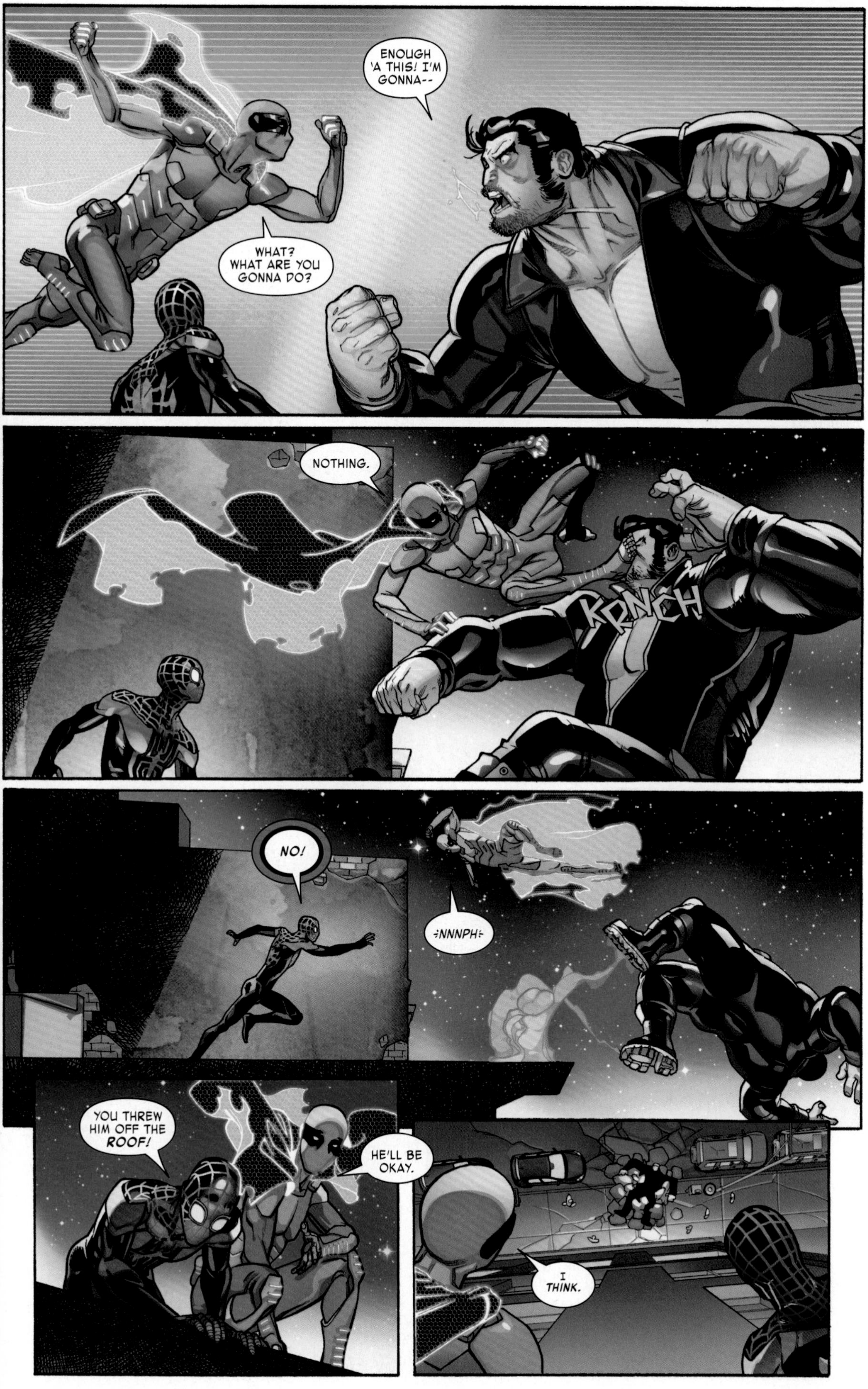
ENOUGH 'A THIS! I'M GONNA--
WHAT? WHAT ARE YOU GONNA DO?
NOTHING.
KRNCH
NO!
NNNPH
YOU THREW HIM OFF THE ROOF!
HE'LL BE OKAY.
I THINK.

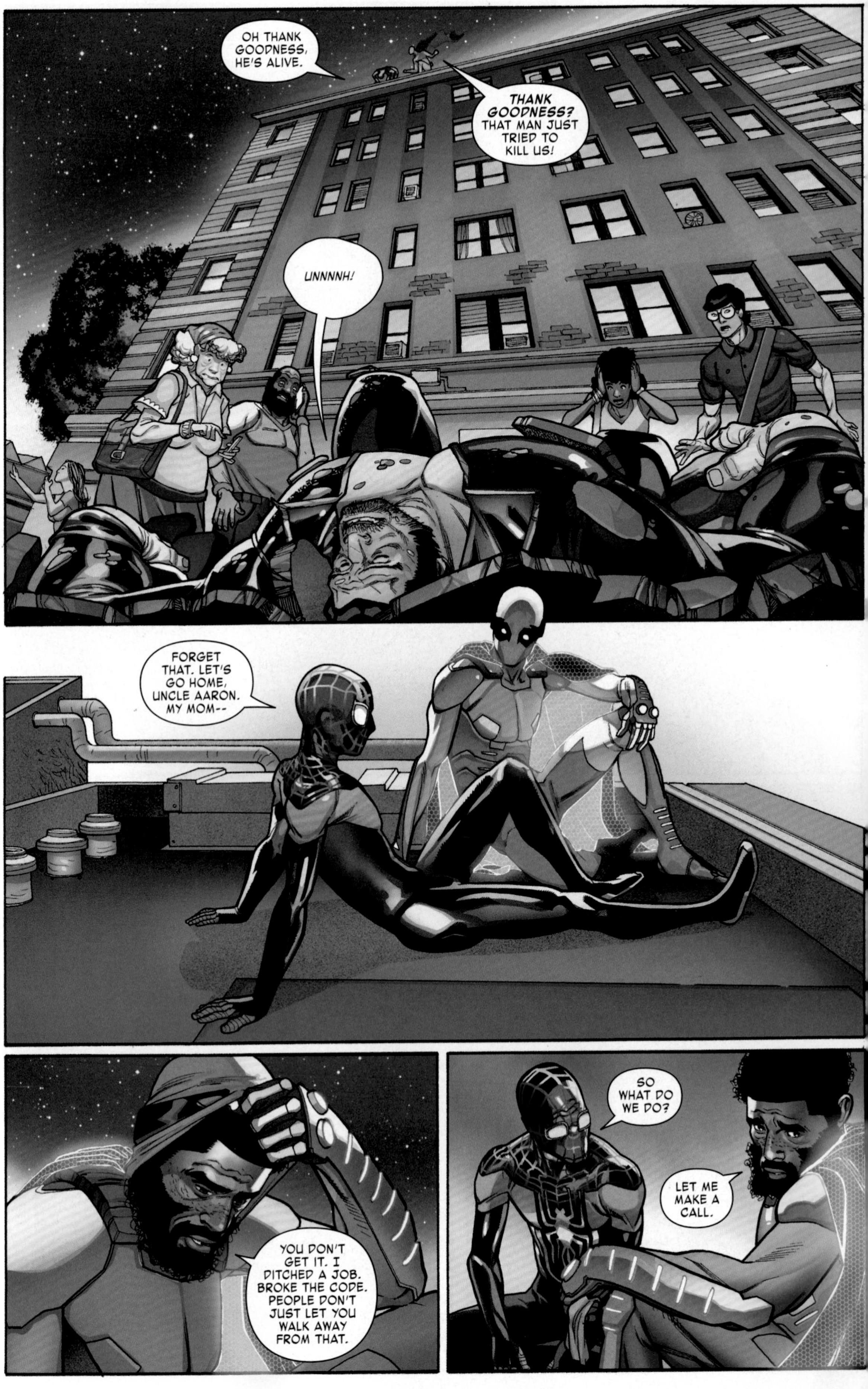
OH THANK GOODNESS, HE'S ALIVE.
THANK GOODNESS? THAT MAN JUST TRIED TO KILL US!
UNNNNH!
FORGET THAT. LET'S GO HOME, UNCLE AARON. MY MOM--
YOU DON'T GET IT. I DITCHED A JOB. BROKE THE CODE. PEOPLE DON'T JUST LET YOU WALK AWAY FROM THAT.
SO WHAT DO WE DO?
LET ME MAKE A CALL.

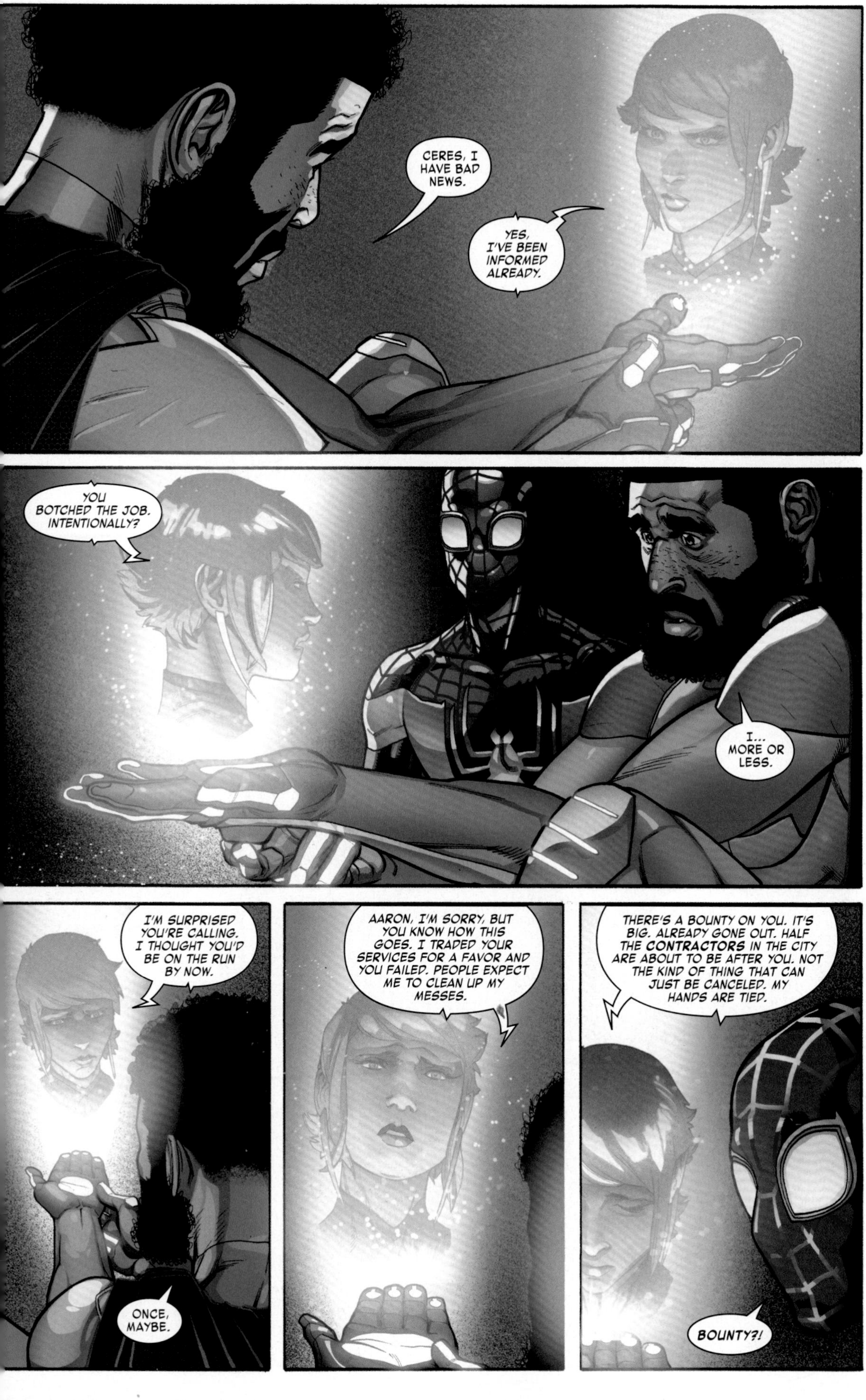
CERES, I HAVE BAD NEWS.
YES, I'VE BEEN INFORMED ALREADY.
YOU BOTCHED THE JOB. INTENTIONALLY?
I... MORE OR LESS.
I'M SURPRISED YOU'RE CALLING. I THOUGHT YOU'D BE ON THE RUN BY NOW.
ONCE, MAYBE.
AARON, I'M SORRY, BUT YOU KNOW HOW THIS GOES. I TRADED YOUR SERVICES FOR A FAVOR AND YOU FAILED. PEOPLE EXPECT ME TO CLEAN UP MY MESSES.
THERE'S A BOUNTY ON YOU. IT'S BIG. ALREADY GONE OUT. HALF THE CONTRACTORS IN THE CITY ARE ABOUT TO BE AFTER YOU. NOT THE KIND OF THING THAT CAN JUST BE CANCELED. MY HANDS ARE TIED.
BOUNTY?!

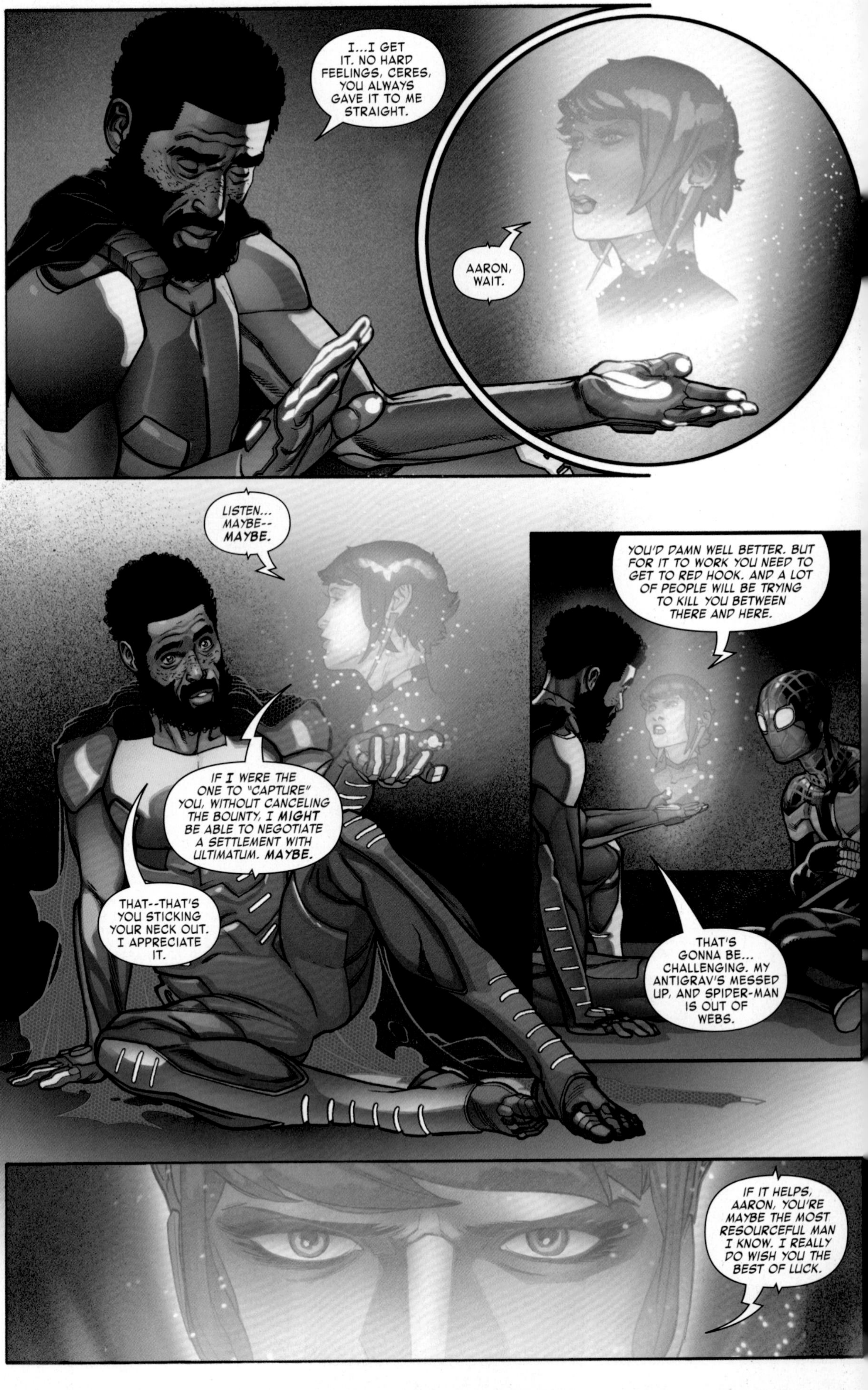

I...I GET IT. NO HARD FEELINGS, CERES, YOU ALWAYS GAVE IT TO ME STRAIGHT.
AARON, WAIT.
LISTEN... MAYBE-- MAYBE.
IF I WERE THE ONE TO "CAPTURE" YOU, WITHOUT CANCELING THE BOUNTY, I MIGHT BE ABLE TO NEGOTIATE A SETTLEMENT WITH ULTIMATUM. MAYBE.
THAT--THAT'S YOU STICKING YOUR NECK OUT. I APPRECIATE IT.
YOU'D DAMN WELL BETTER. BUT FOR IT TO WORK YOU NEED TO GET TO RED HOOK. AND A LOT OF PEOPLE WILL BE TRYING TO KILL YOU BETWEEN THERE AND HERE.
THAT'S GONNA BE... CHALLENGING. MY ANTIGRAV'S MESSED UP, AND SPIDER-MAN IS OUT OF WEBS.
IF IT HELPS, AARON, YOU'RE MAYBE THE MOST RESOURCEFUL MAN I KNOW. I REALLY DO WISH YOU THE BEST OF LUCK.

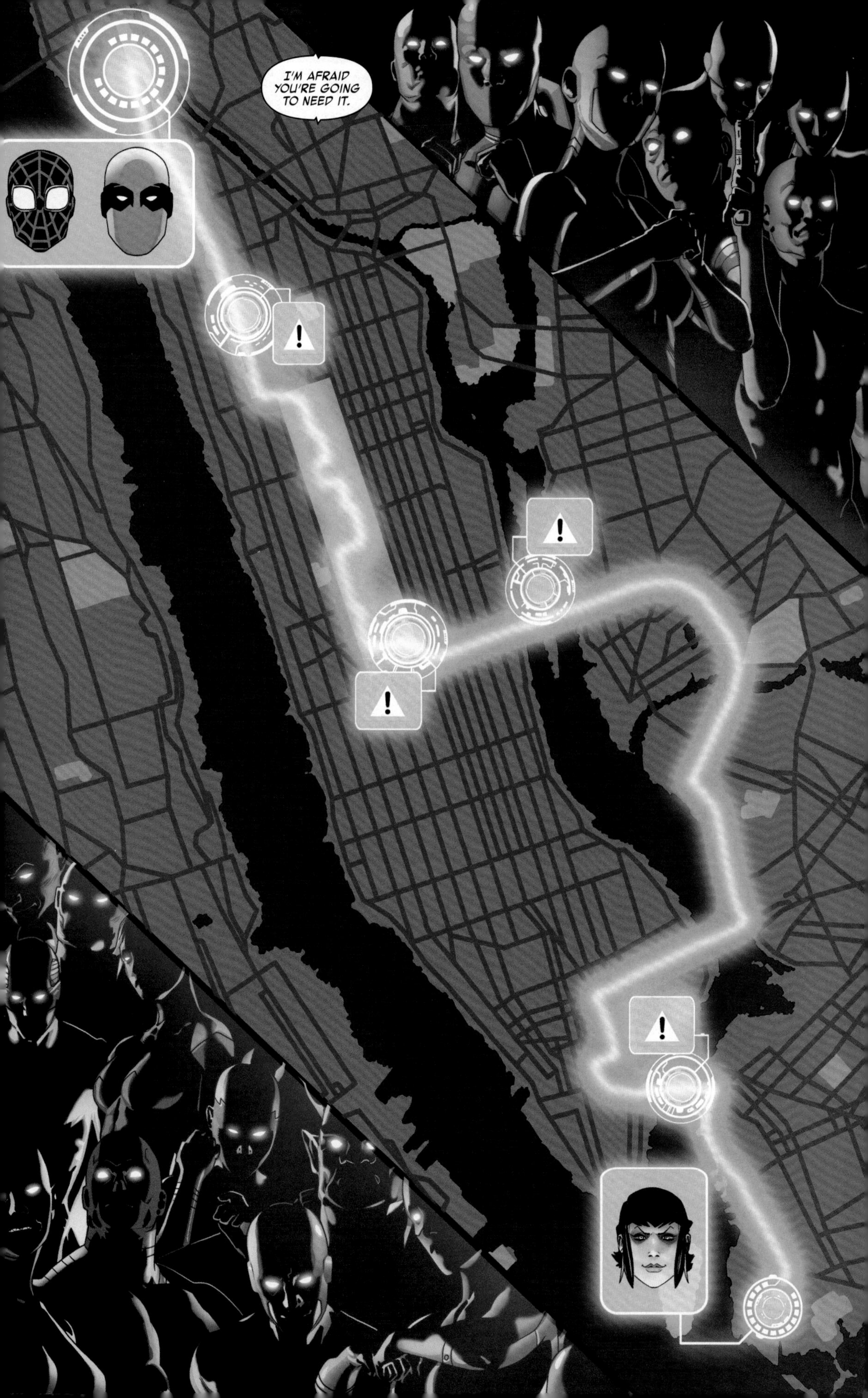
I'M AFRAID YOU'RE GOING TO NEED IT.

13

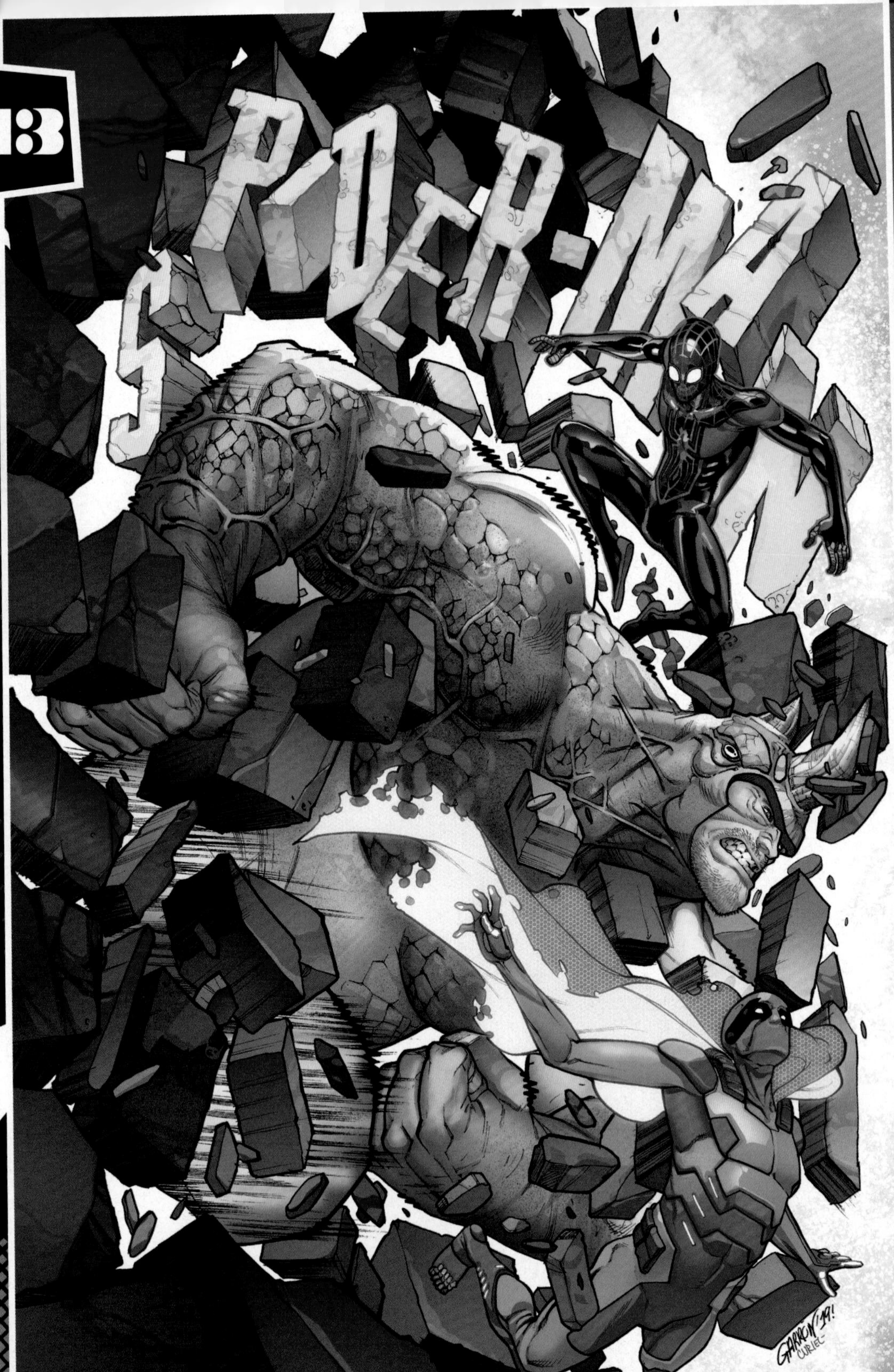

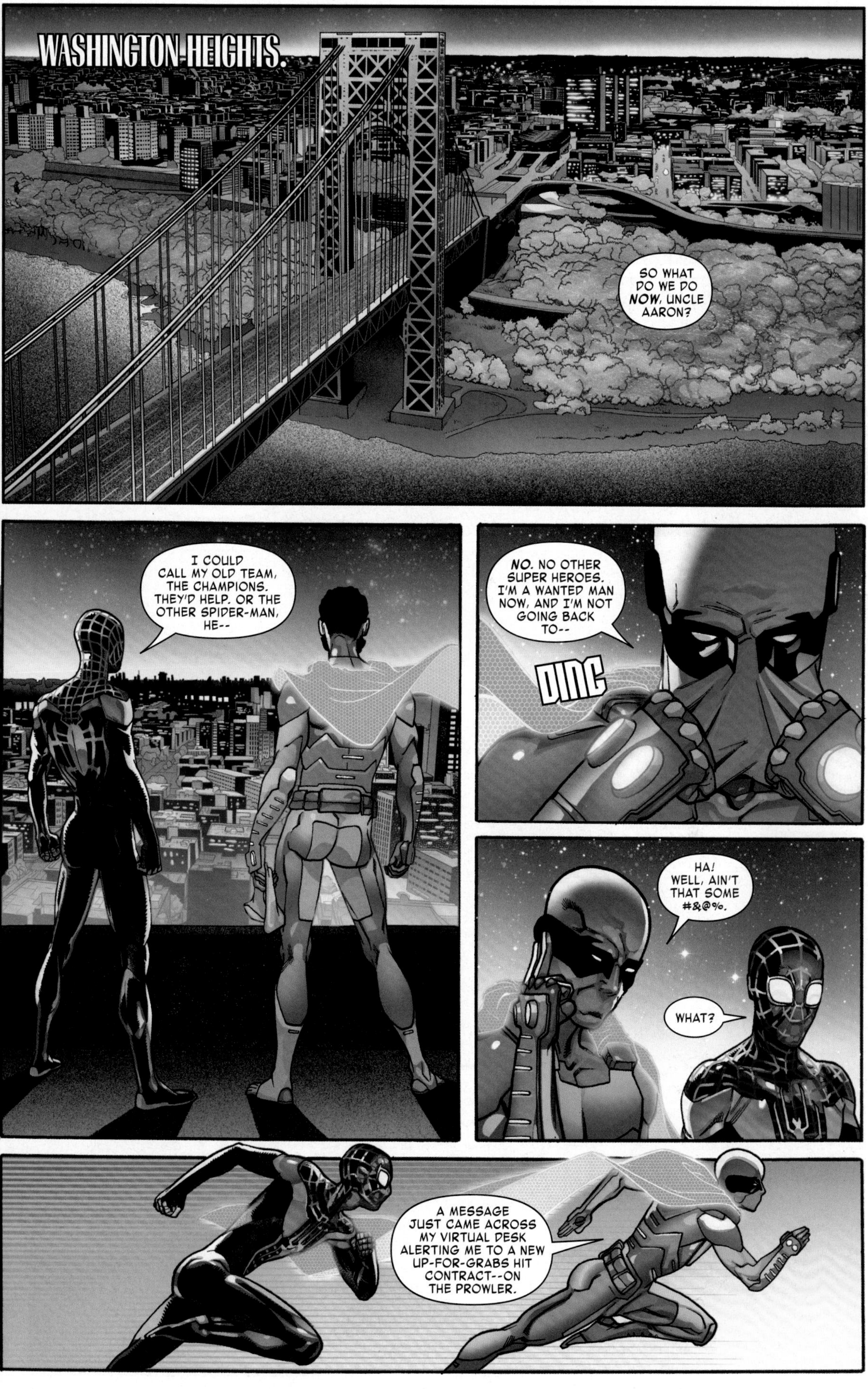
WASHINGTON HEIGHTS.
SO WHAT DO WE DO NOW, UNCLE AARON?
I COULD CALL MY OLD TEAM, THE CHAMPIONS. THEY'D HELP. OR THE OTHER SPIDER-MAN, HE--
NO. NO OTHER SUPER HEROES. I'M A WANTED MAN NOW, AND I'M NOT GOING BACK TO--
DING
HA! WELL, AIN'T THAT SOME #&@%.
WHAT?
A MESSAGE JUST CAME ACROSS MY VIRTUAL DESK ALERTING ME TO A NEW UP-FOR-GRABS HIT CONTRACT--ON THE PROWLER.

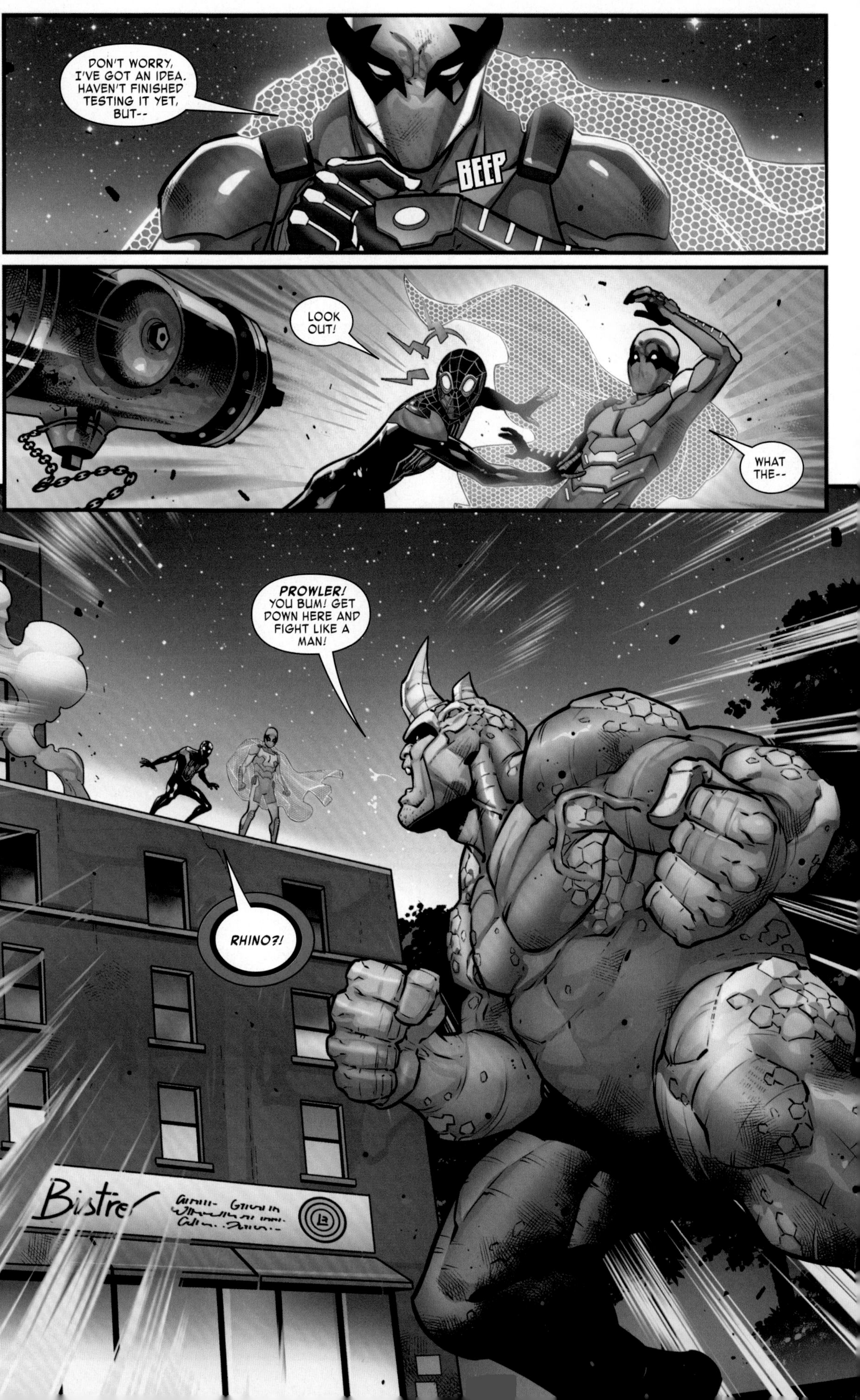

DON'T WORRY, I'VE GOT AN IDEA. HAVEN'T FINISHED TESTING IT YET, BUT--
BEEP
LOOK OUT!
WHAT THE--
PROWLER! YOU BUM! GET DOWN HERE AND FIGHT LIKE A MAN!
RHINO?!
Bistre

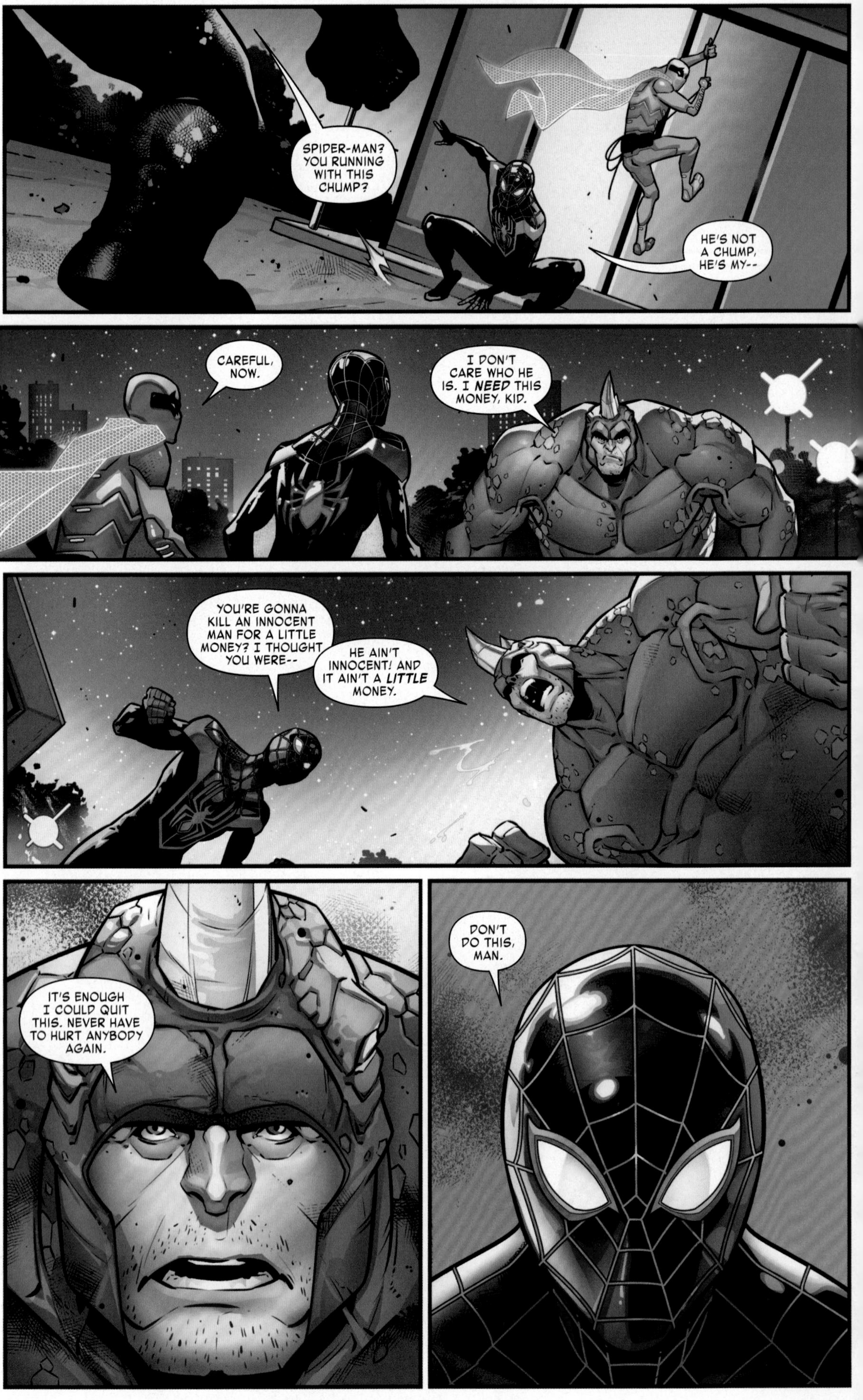
SPIDER-MAN? YOU RUNNING WITH THIS CHUMP?
HE'S NOT A CHUMP, HE'S MY--
CAREFUL, NOW.
I DON'T CARE WHO HE IS. I NEED THIS MONEY, KID.
YOU'RE GONNA KILL AN INNOCENT MAN FOR A LITTLE MONEY? I THOUGHT YOU WERE--
HE AIN'T INNOCENT! AND IT AIN'T A LITTLE MONEY.
IT'S ENOUGH I COULD QUIT THIS. NEVER HAVE TO HURT ANYBODY AGAIN.
DON'T DO THIS, MAN.

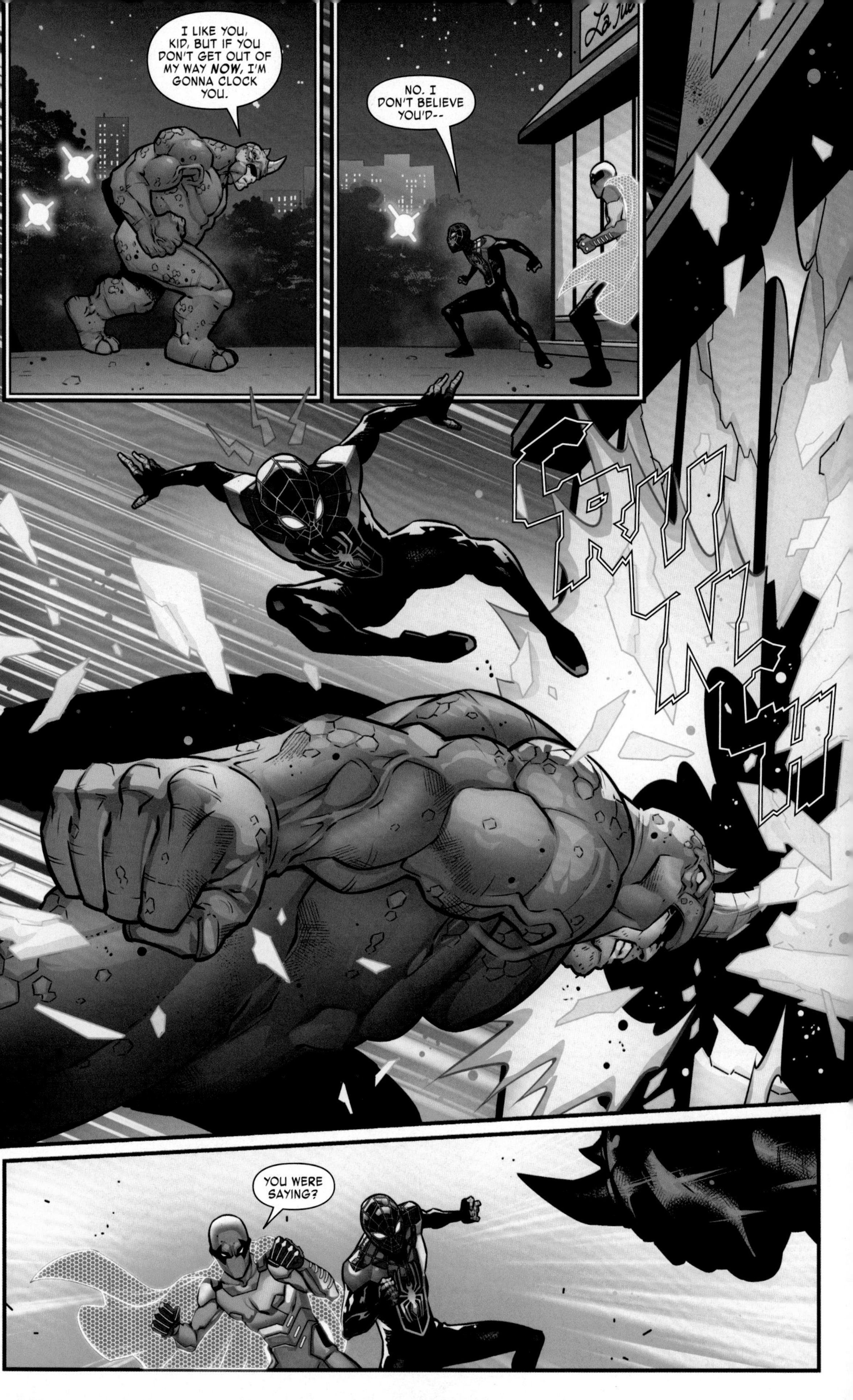
I LIKE YOU, KID, BUT IF YOU DON'T GET OUT OF MY WAY NOW, I'M GONNA CLOCK YOU.
NO. I DON'T BELIEVE YOU'D--
YOU WERE SAYING?

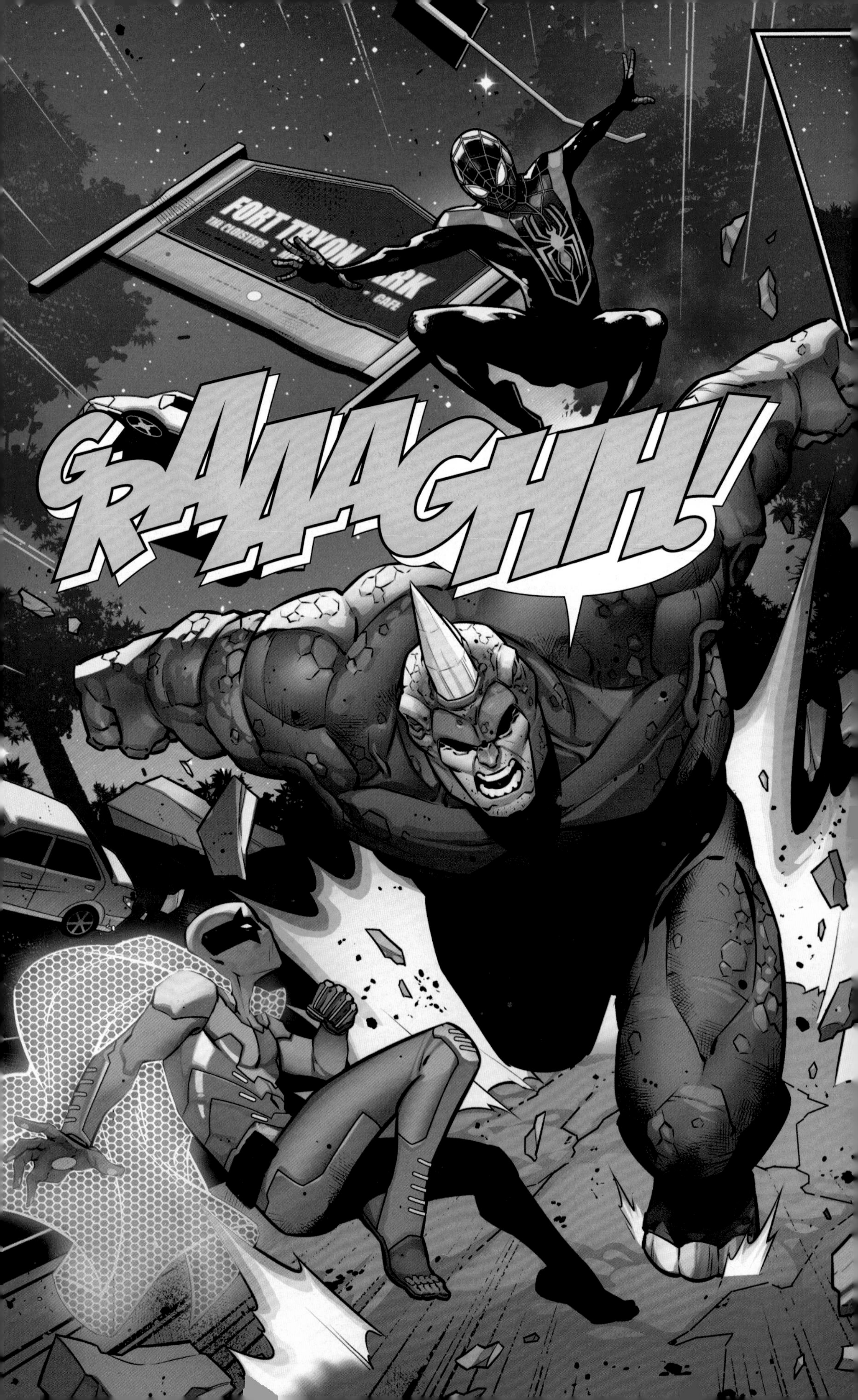
FORT TRYON
THE CLOISTERS
CAFE
GRAAAGHH!

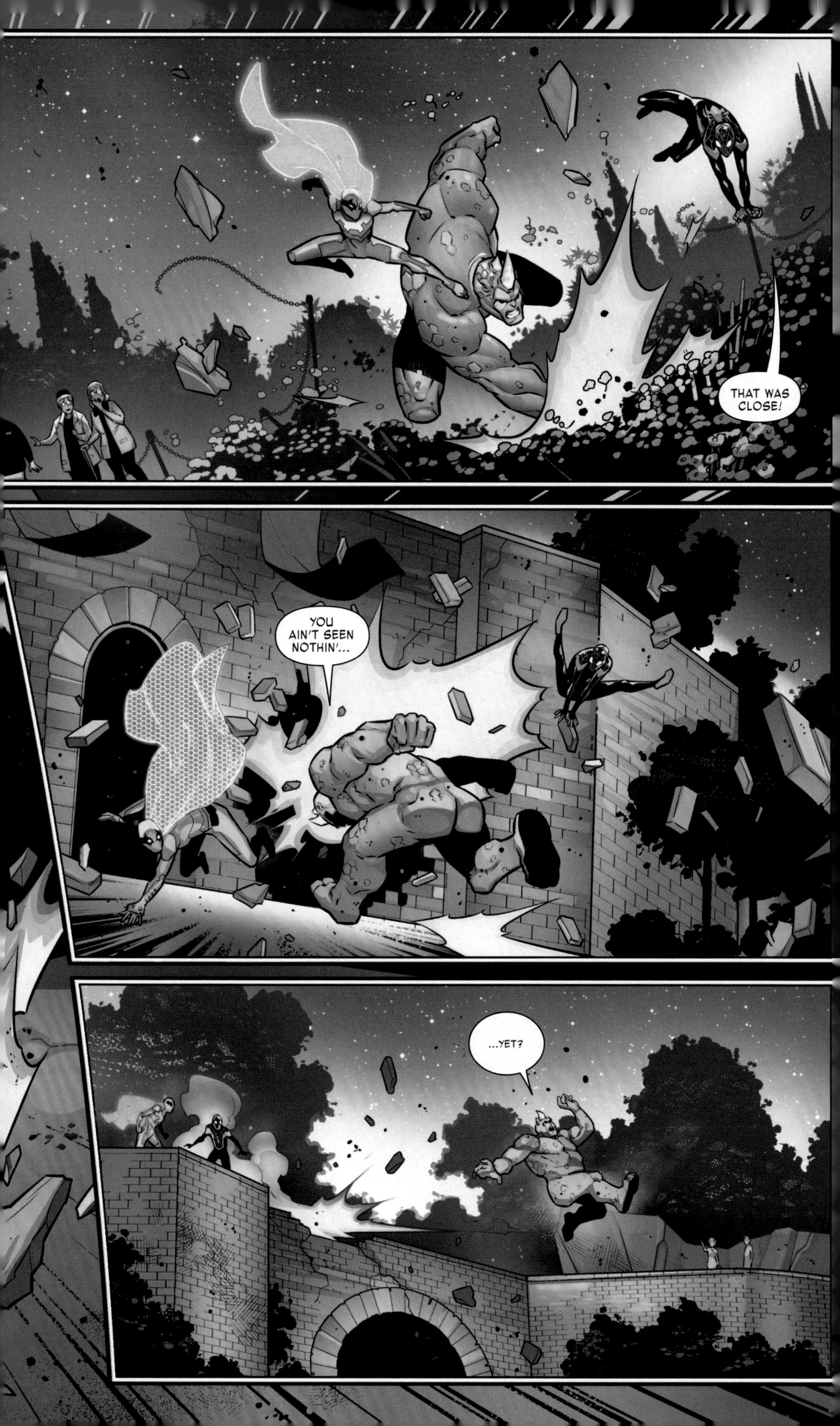
THAT WAS CLOSE!
YOU AIN'T SEEN NOTHIN'...
...YET?

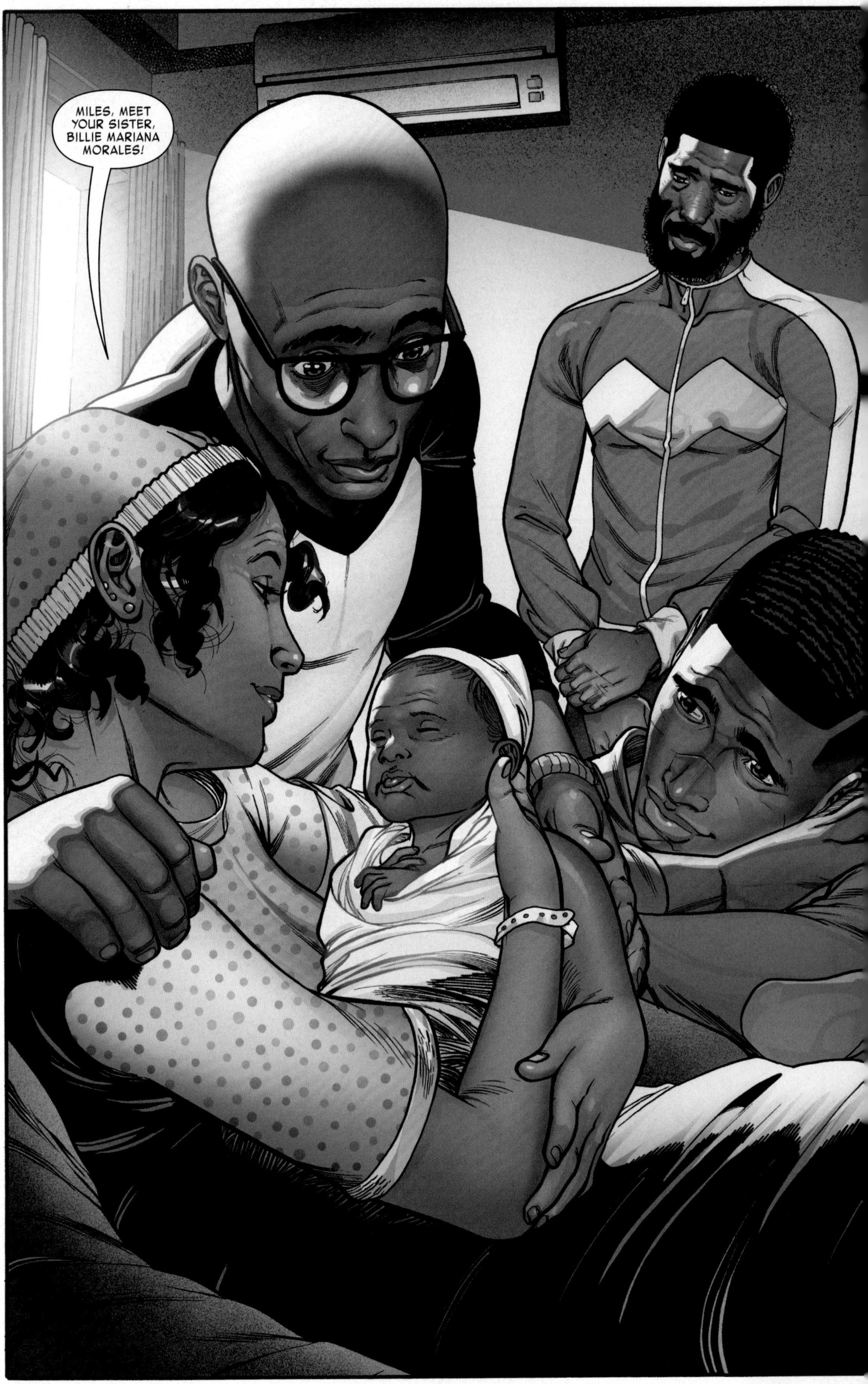
MILES, MEET YOUR SISTER, BILLIE MARIANA MORALES!

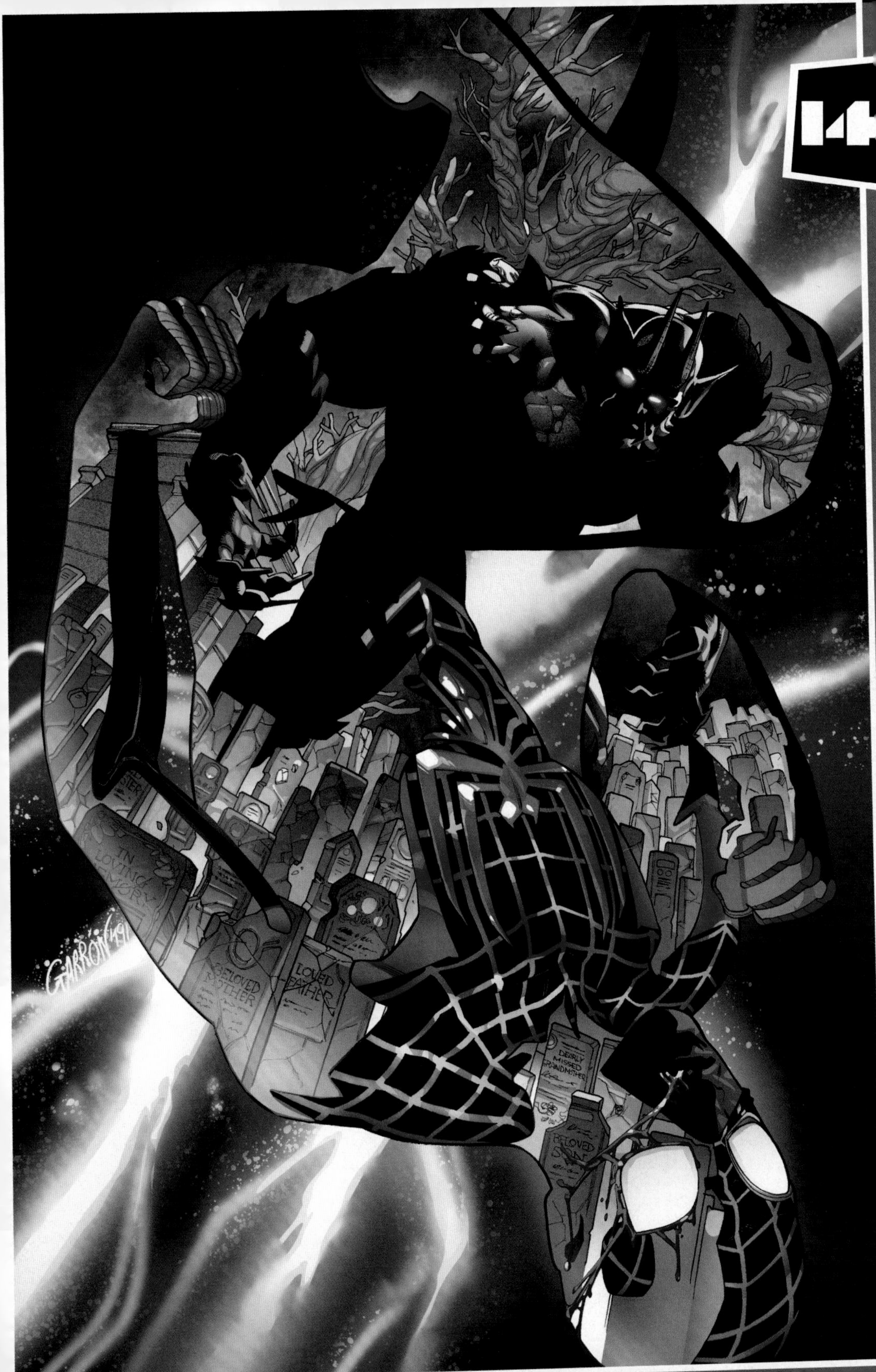
IN LOVING
BELOVED MOTHER
LOVED FATHER
DEARLY MISSED GRANDMOTHER
GARRON '19

14

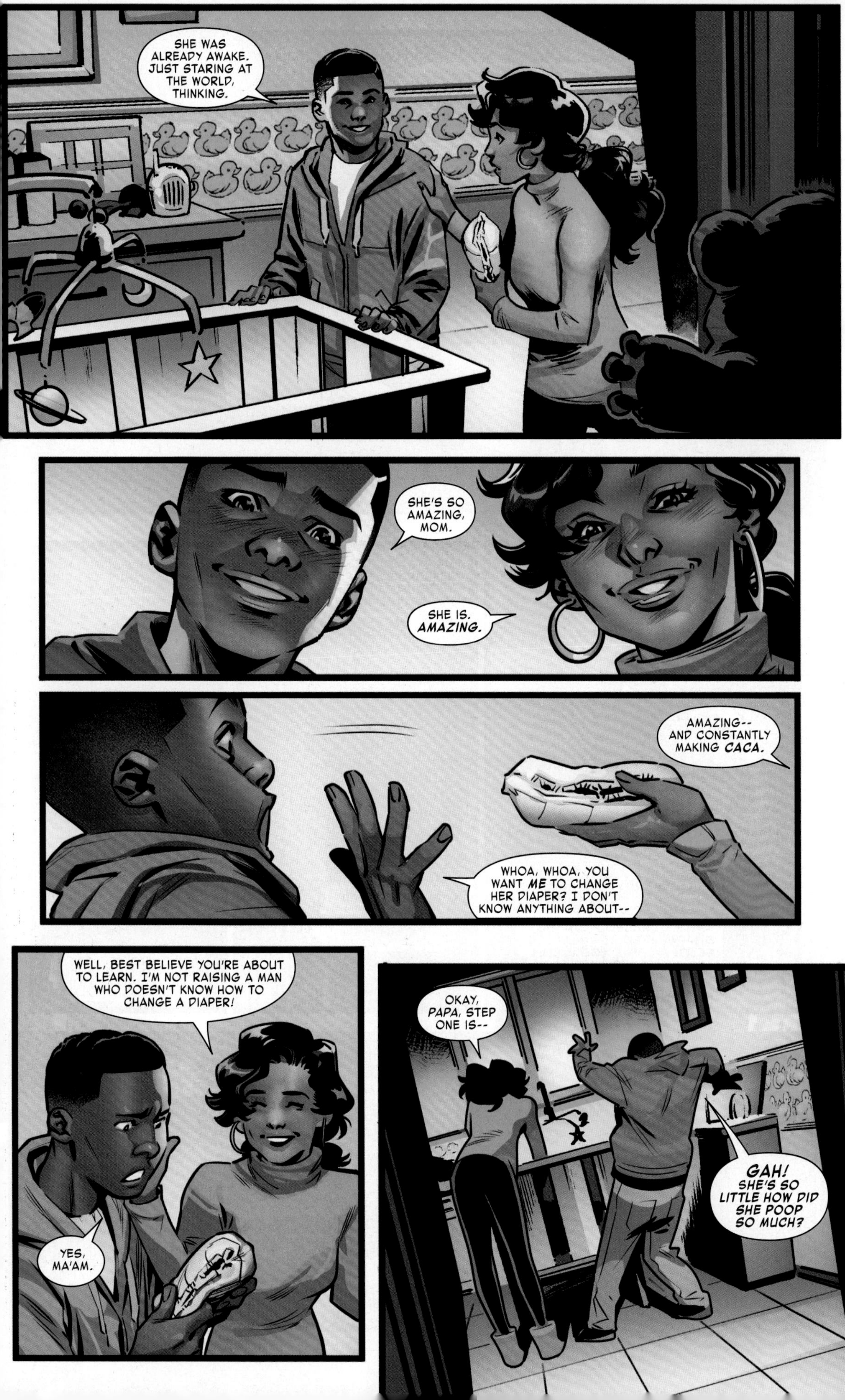
SHE WAS ALREADY AWAKE. JUST STARING AT THE WORLD, THINKING.
SHE'S SO AMAZING, MOM.
SHE IS. **AMAZING.**
AMAZING-- AND CONSTANTLY MAKING **CACA.**
WHOA, WHOA, YOU WANT **ME** TO CHANGE HER DIAPER? I DON'T KNOW ANYTHING ABOUT--
WELL, BEST BELIEVE YOU'RE ABOUT TO LEARN. I'M NOT RAISING A MAN WHO DOESN'T KNOW HOW TO CHANGE A DIAPER!
YES, MA'AM.
OKAY, **PAPA,** STEP ONE IS--
GAH! SHE'S SO LITTLE HOW DID SHE POOP SO MUCH?

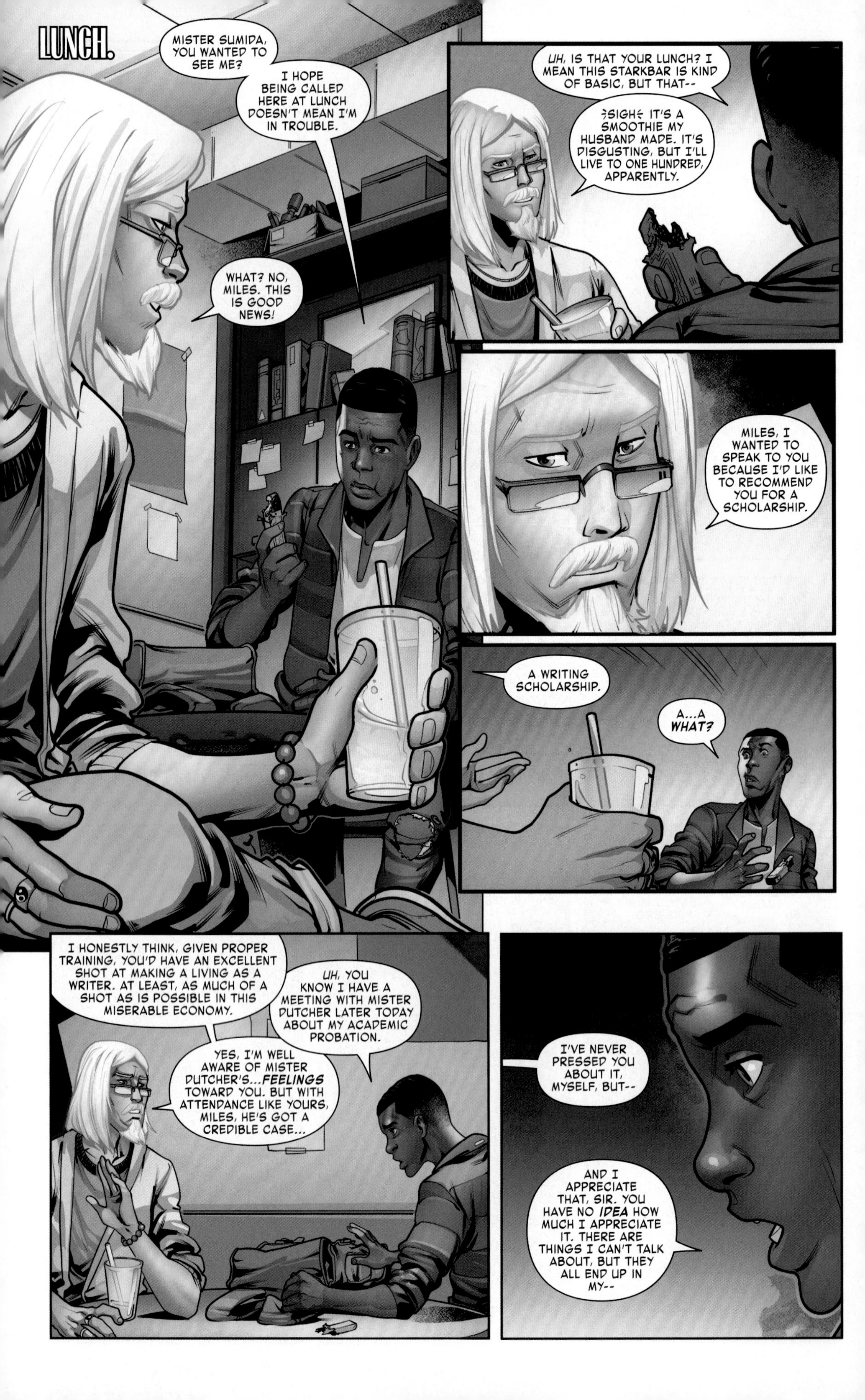
LUNCH.
MISTER SUMIDA, YOU WANTED TO SEE ME?
I HOPE BEING CALLED HERE AT LUNCH DOESN'T MEAN I'M IN TROUBLE.
WHAT? NO, MILES. THIS IS GOOD NEWS!
UH, IS THAT YOUR LUNCH? I MEAN THIS STARKBAR IS KIND OF BASIC, BUT THAT--
SIGH IT'S A SMOOTHIE MY HUSBAND MADE. IT'S DISGUSTING, BUT I'LL LIVE TO ONE HUNDRED, APPARENTLY.
MILES, I WANTED TO SPEAK TO YOU BECAUSE I'D LIKE TO RECOMMEND YOU FOR A SCHOLARSHIP.
A WRITING SCHOLARSHIP.
A...A WHAT?
I HONESTLY THINK, GIVEN PROPER TRAINING, YOU'D HAVE AN EXCELLENT SHOT AT MAKING A LIVING AS A WRITER. AT LEAST, AS MUCH OF A SHOT AS IS POSSIBLE IN THIS MISERABLE ECONOMY.
UH, YOU KNOW I HAVE A MEETING WITH MISTER DUTCHER LATER TODAY ABOUT MY ACADEMIC PROBATION.
YES, I'M WELL AWARE OF MISTER DUTCHER'S...FEELINGS TOWARD YOU. BUT WITH ATTENDANCE LIKE YOURS, MILES, HE'S GOT A CREDIBLE CASE...
I'VE NEVER PRESSED YOU ABOUT IT, MYSELF, BUT--
AND I APPRECIATE THAT, SIR. YOU HAVE NO IDEA HOW MUCH I APPRECIATE IT. THERE ARE THINGS I CAN'T TALK ABOUT, BUT THEY ALL END UP IN MY--

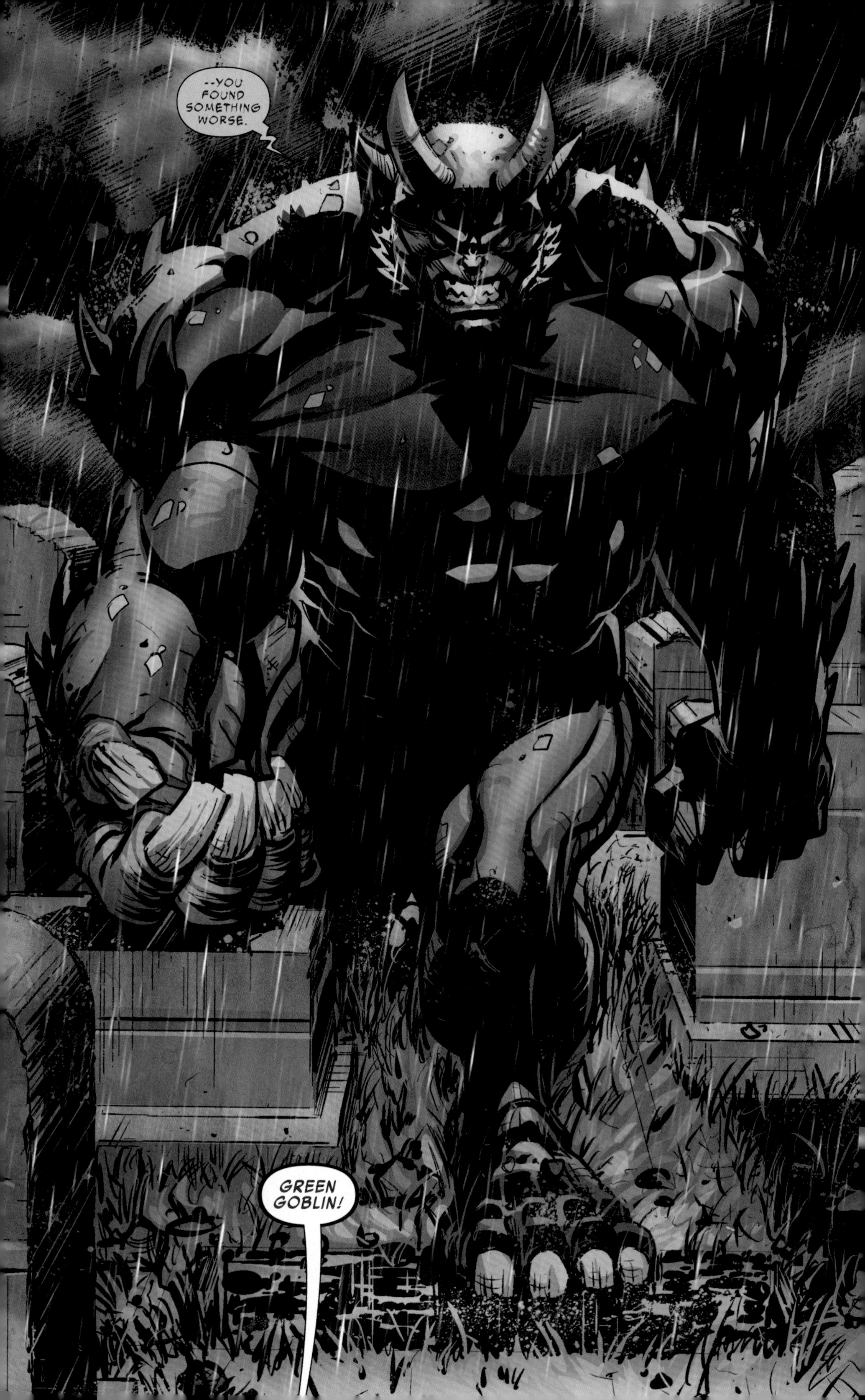
--YOU FOUND SOMETHING WORSE.
GREEN GOBLIN!

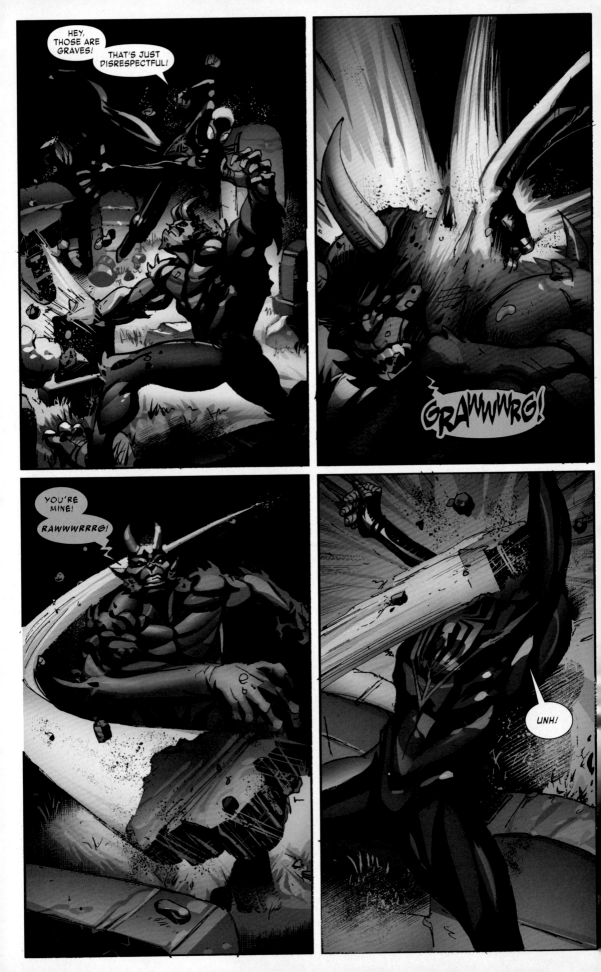

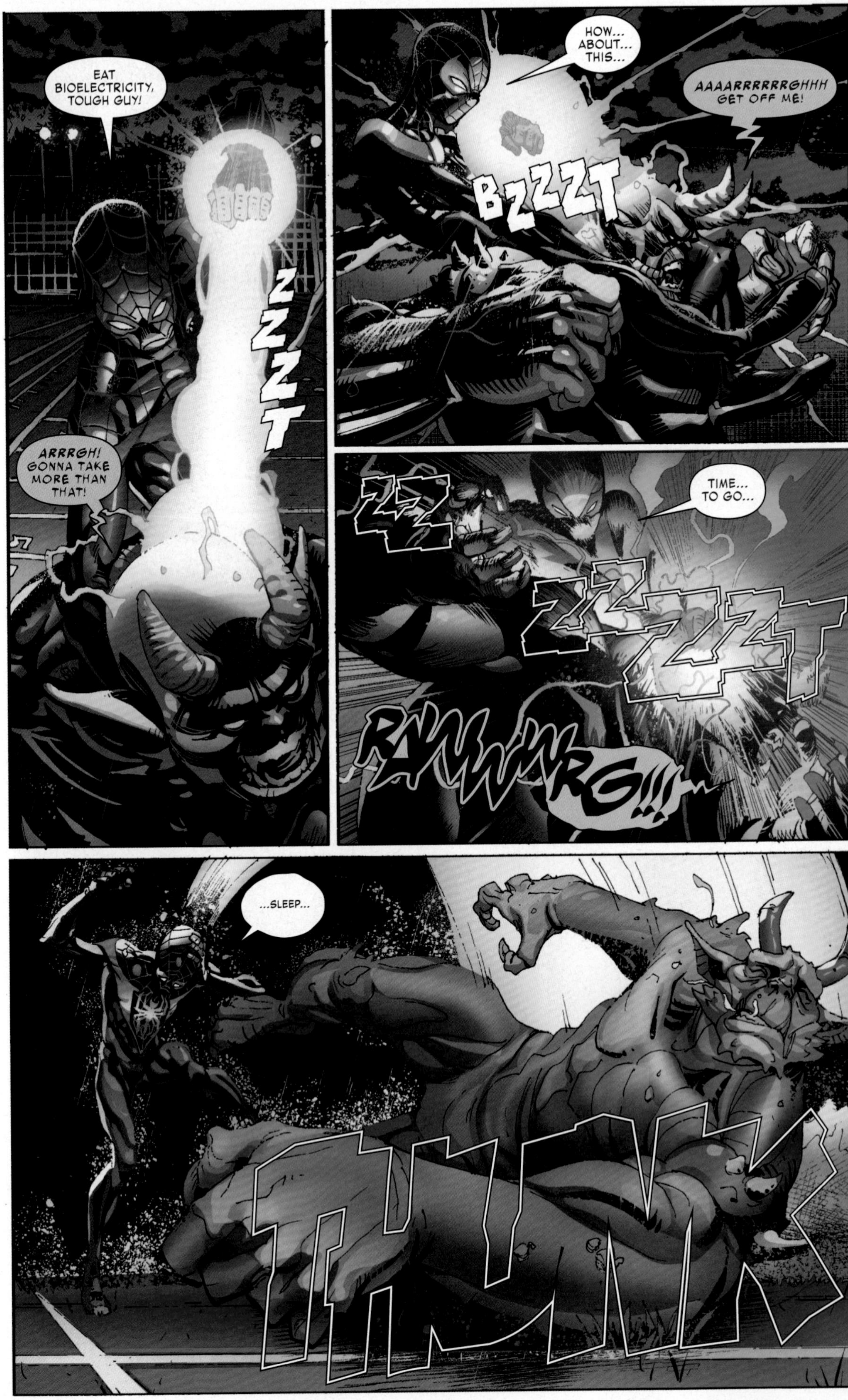
EAT BIOELECTRICITY, TOUGH GUY!
ZZZZT
ARRRGH! GONNA TAKE MORE THAN THAT!
HOW... ABOUT... THIS...
AAAARRRRRRGHHH GET OFF ME!
BZZZT
TIME... TO GO...
...SLEEP...

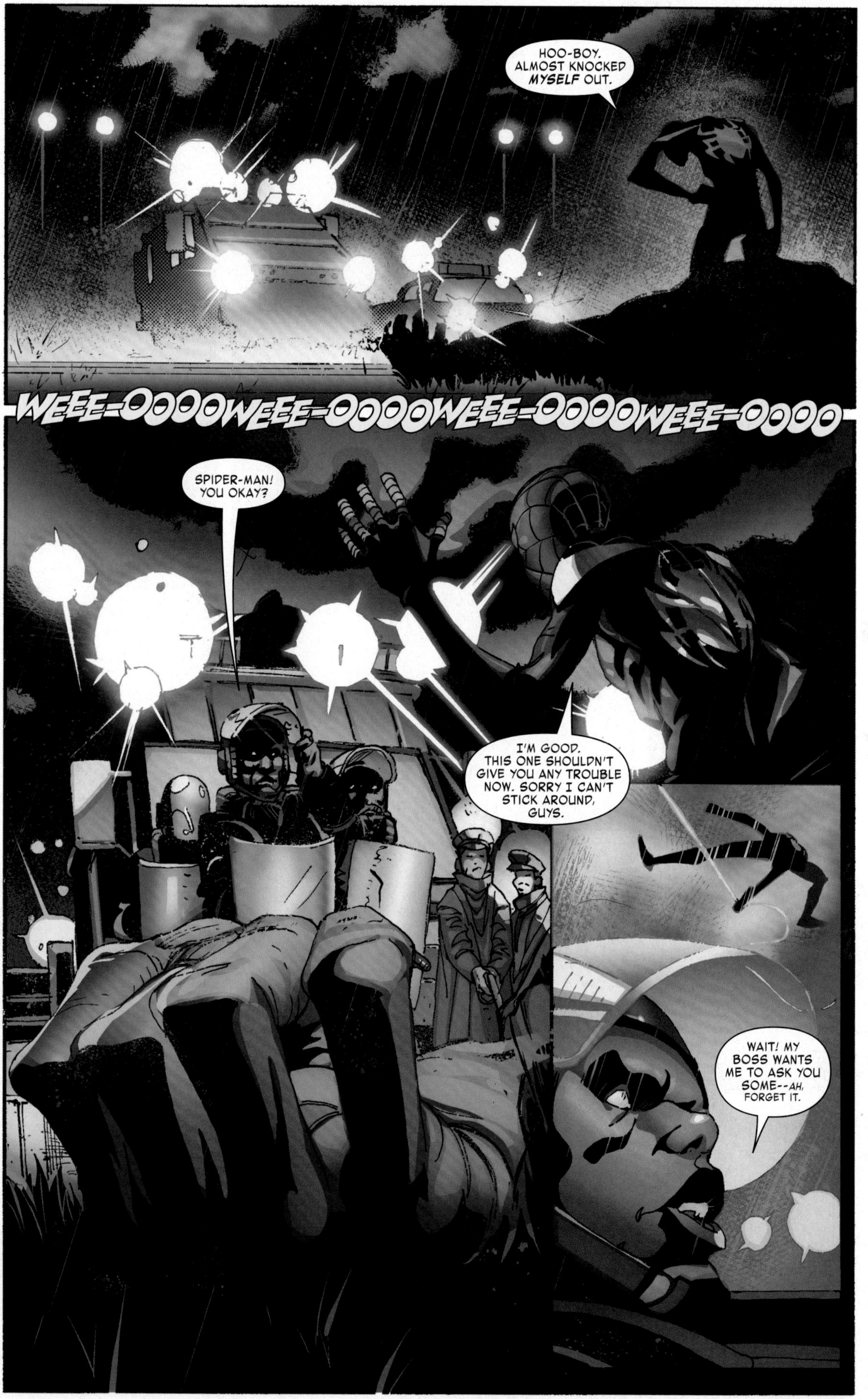
HOO-BOY. ALMOST KNOCKED MYSELF OUT.
WEEE-OOOOWEEE-OOOOWEEE-OOOOWEEE-OOOO
SPIDER-MAN! YOU OKAY?
I'M GOOD. THIS ONE SHOULDN'T GIVE YOU ANY TROUBLE NOW. SORRY I CAN'T STICK AROUND, GUYS.
WAIT! MY BOSS WANTS ME TO ASK YOU SOME--AH, FORGET IT.

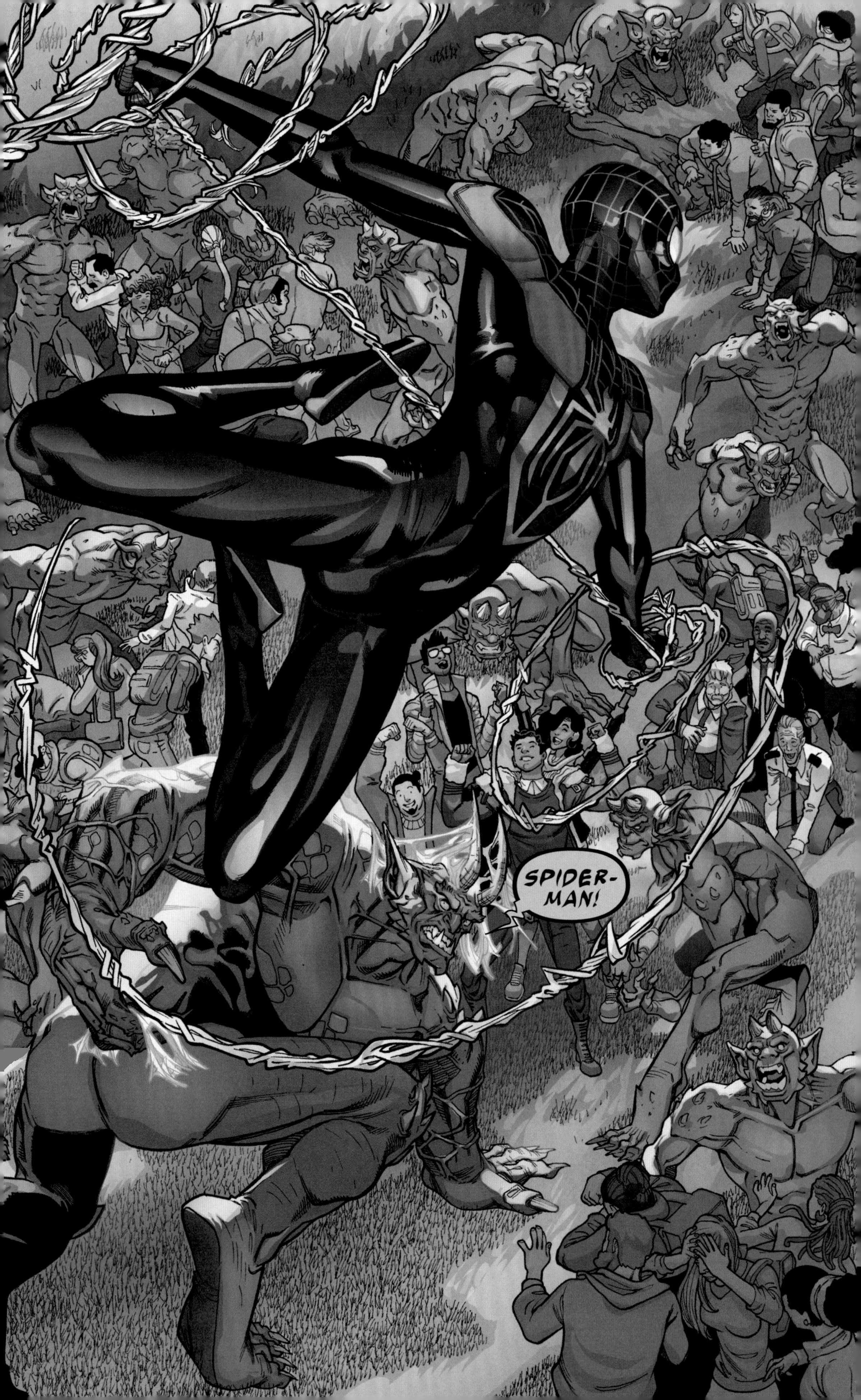
SPIDER-MAN!

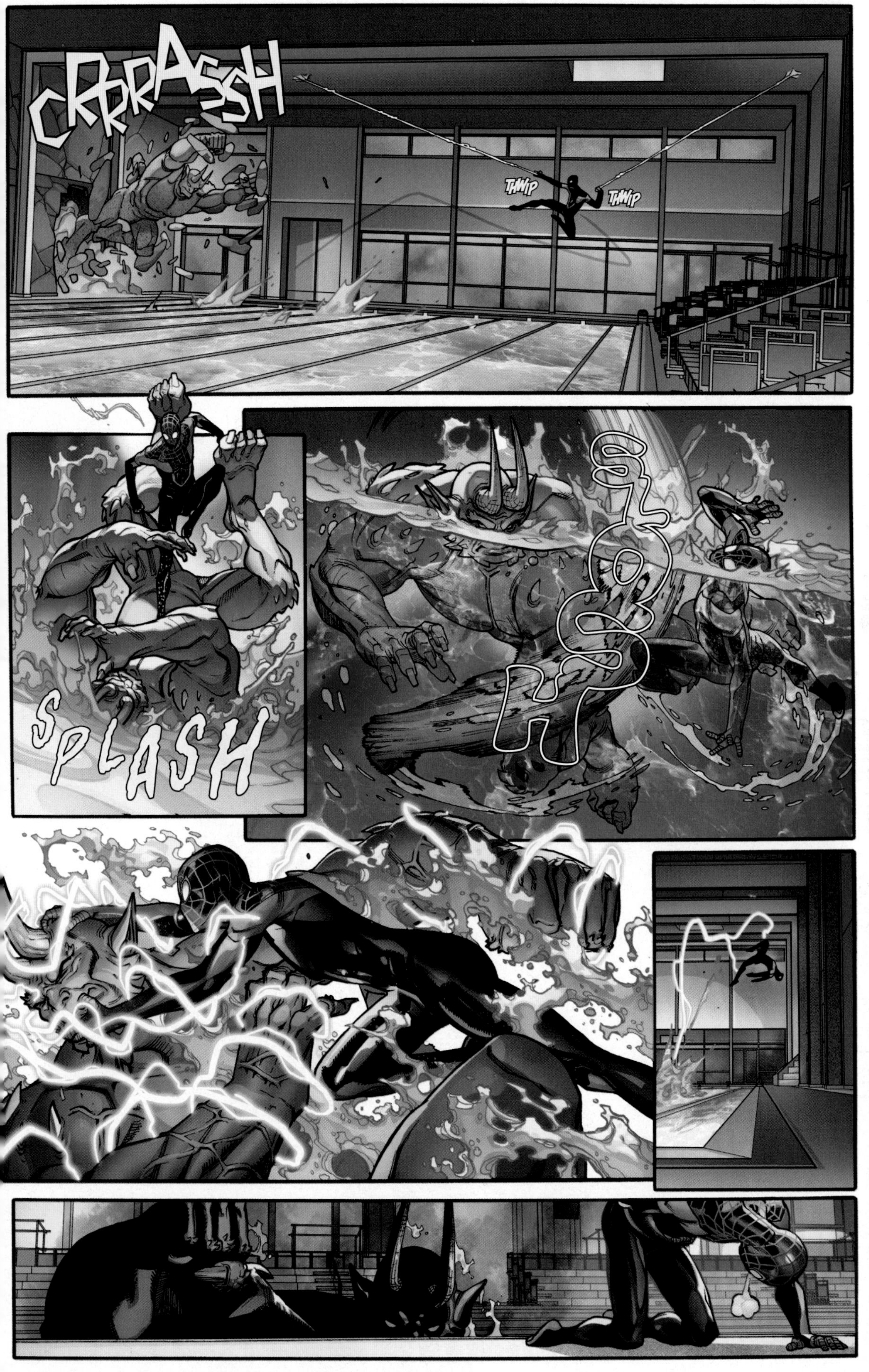
CRRRASSH
THWIP
THWIP
SPLASH

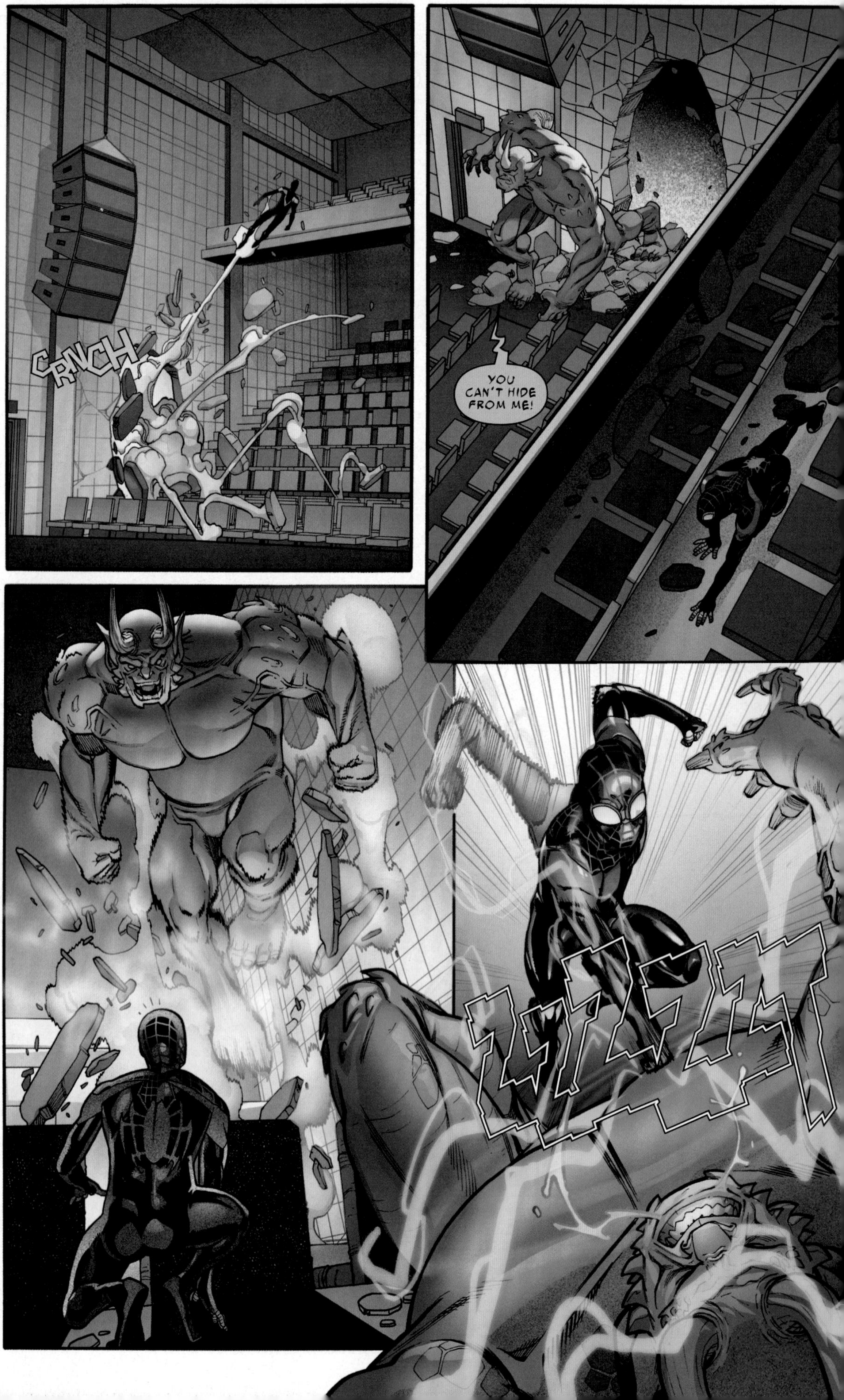
CRNCH
YOU CAN'T HIDE FROM ME!

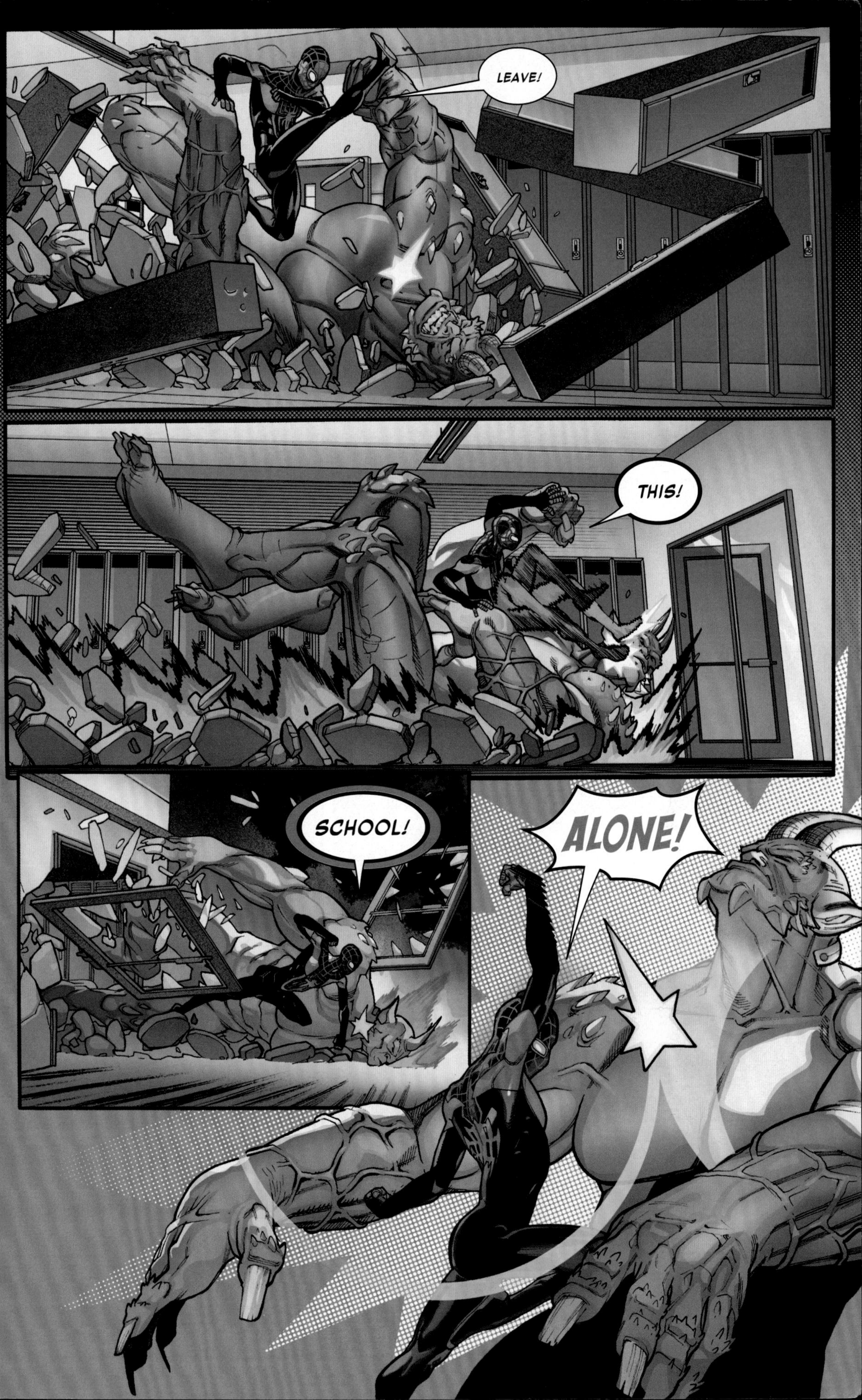
LEAVE!
THIS!
SCHOOL!
ALONE!

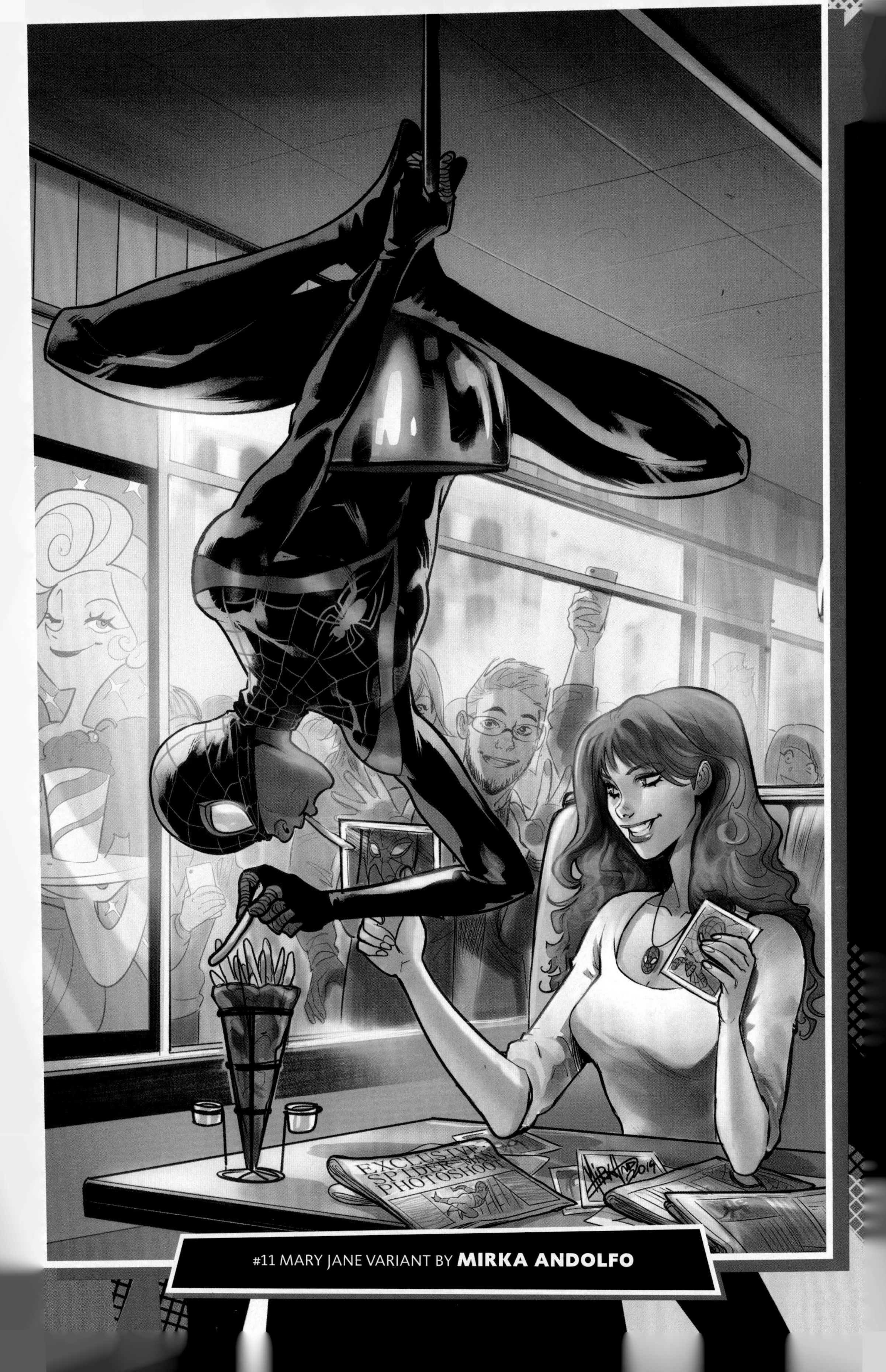
EXCLUSIVE
PHOTOSHOOT

#11 MARY JANE VARIANT BY **MIRKA ANDOLFO**

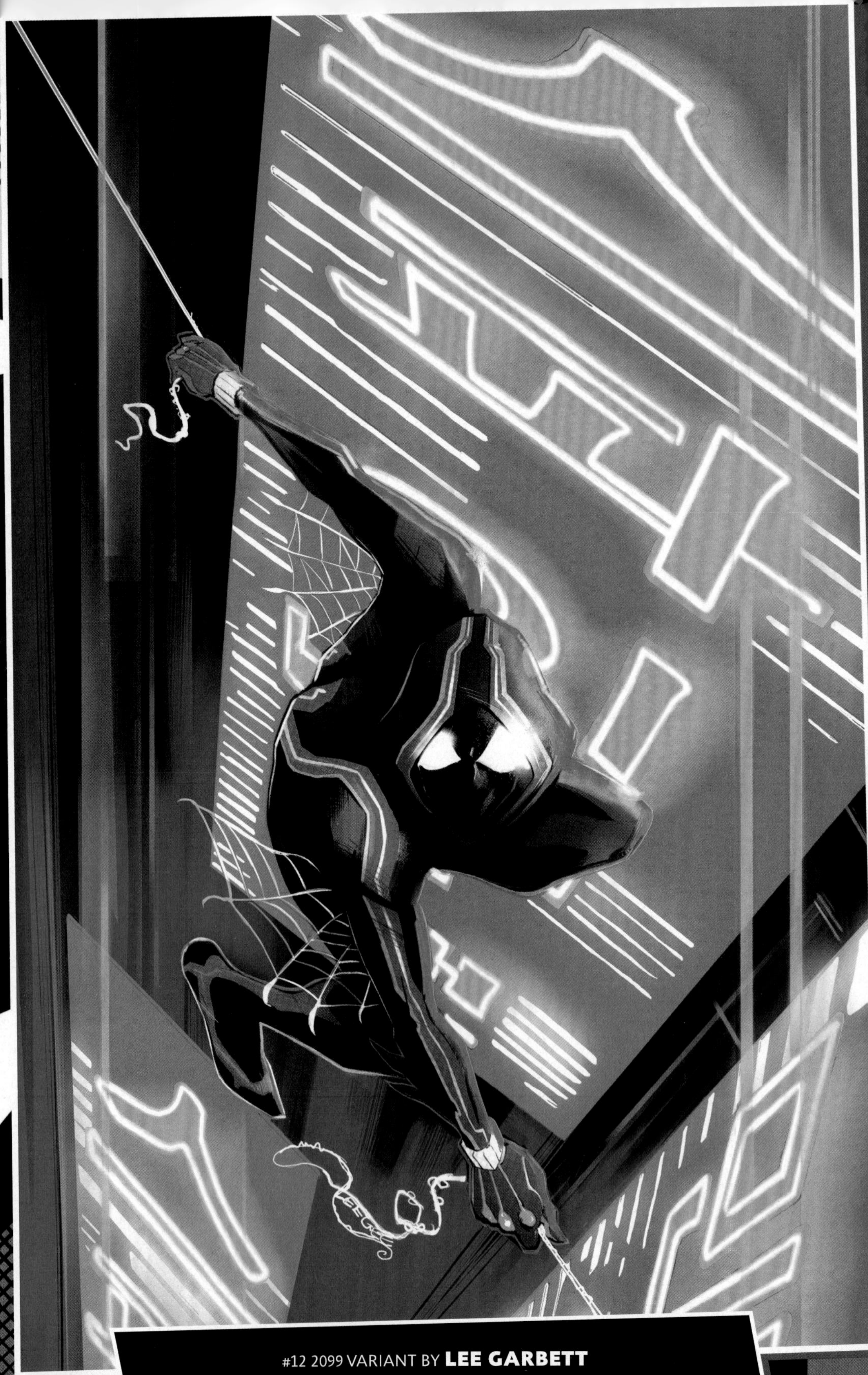

#12 2099 VARIANT BY **LEE GARBETT**

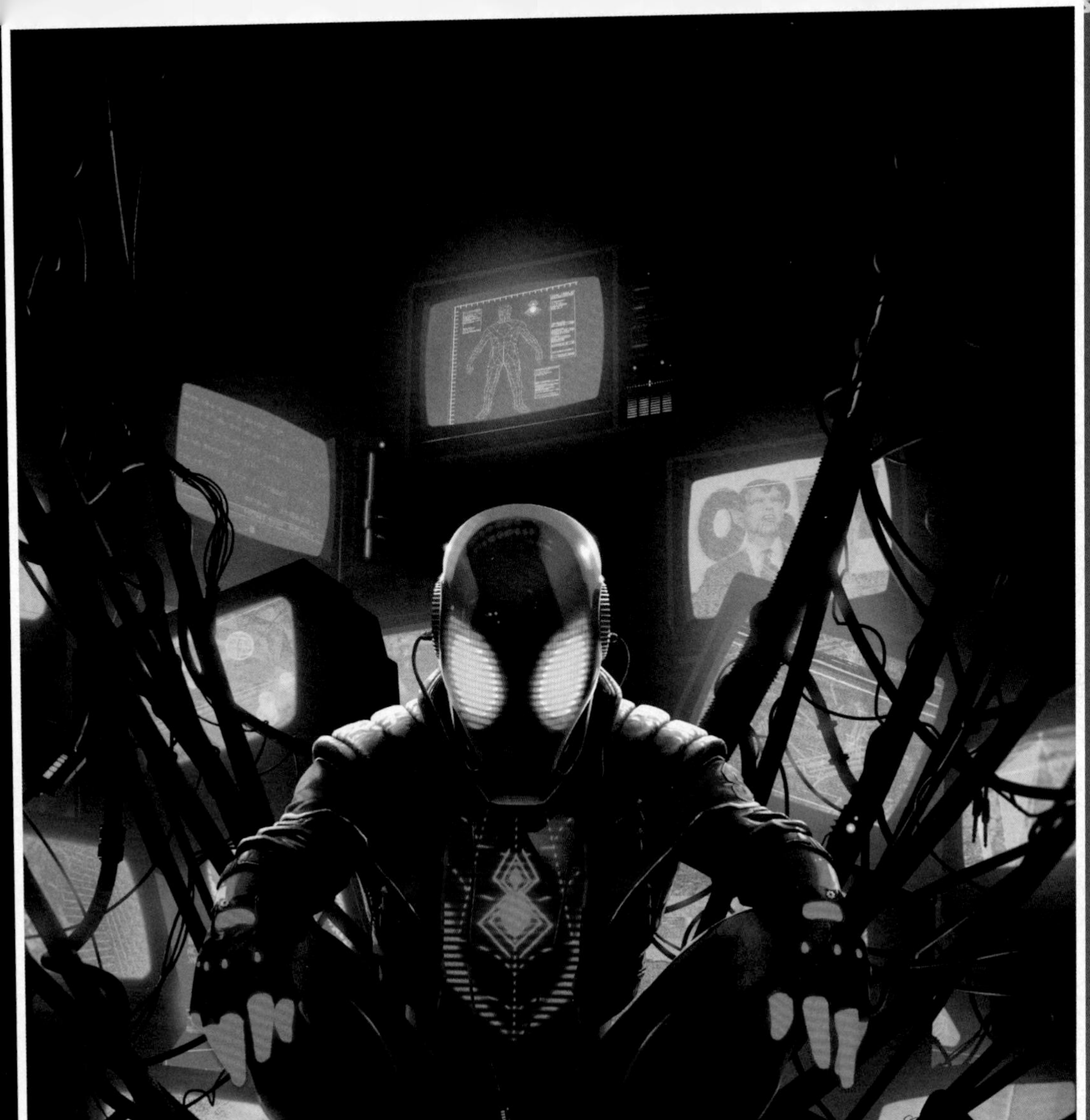

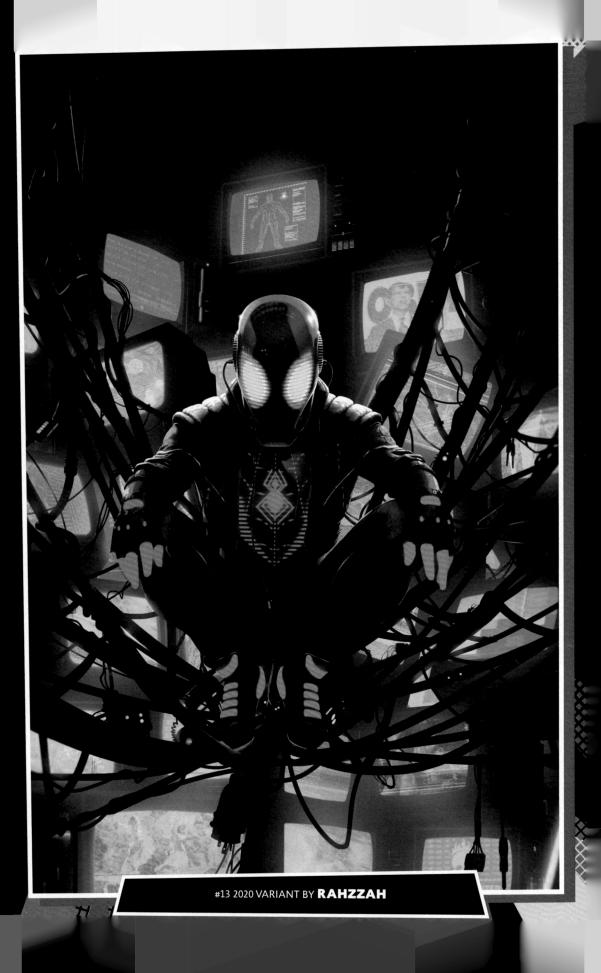

#13 2020 VARIANT BY **RAHZZAH**

#13 VENOM ISLAND VARIANT BY
EDUARD PETROVICH

#14 MARVELS X VARIANT BY
DECLAN SHALVEY

#15 GWEN STACY VARIANT BY
NICK BRADSHAW &
ERICK ARCINIEGA